JOE PAPR...

PREPARING HEARTS AND MINDS

9 SIMPLE WAYS FOR CATECHISTS TO CULTIVATE A LIVING FAITH

LOYOLAPRESS.
A JESUIT MINISTRY
Chicago

LOYOLA PRESS.
A JESUIT MINISTRY

3441 N. Ashland Avenue
Chicago, Illinois 60657
(800) 621-1008
www.loyolapress.com

Cover and interior design by Loyola Press
Cover art credit: Yasonya/iStockphoto/Getty Images, natrot/iStockphoto/Getty Images, and rimglow/iStockphoto/Getty Images.

Cartoons by Leighton Drake
Cartoons © 2020 Loyola Press

Unless otherwise indicated, Scripture quotations are from Holy Bible, New International Version®, NIV® Copyright ©1973, 1978, 1984, 2011 by Biblica, Inc.® Used by permission. All rights reserved worldwide.

ISBN-13: 978-0-8294-5003-3
Library of Congress Control Number: 2020934389

Printed in the United States of America
20 21 22 23 24 25 26 27 28 29 LSC 10 9 8 7 6 5 4 3 2 1

DEDICATION

I dedicate this book to Barbara and Jim Campbell, who taught me how to till the soil, plant the seeds of God's Word, nurture growth, and reap the harvest.

Other Loyola Press Books by Joe Paprocki

*The Catechist's Toolbox: How to Thrive
as a Religious Education Teacher*

*A Well-Built Faith: A Catholic's Guide to
Knowing and Sharing What We Believe*

*The Bible Blueprint: A Catholic's Guide to
Understanding and Embracing God's Word*

*Living the Mass: How One Hour a Week Can
Change Your Life (with Fr. Dominic Grassi)*

*Practice Makes Catholic: Moving from
a Learned Faith to a Lived Faith*

*Beyond the Catechist's Toolbox: Catechesis That
Not Only Informs but Also Transforms*

*7 Keys to Spiritual Wellness: Enriching Your Faith
by Strengthening the Health of Your Soul*

*Under the Influence of Jesus: The Transforming
Experience of Encountering Christ*

*The Catechist's Backpack: Spiritual Essentials
for the Journey*

*A Church on the Move: 52 Ways to Get
Mission and Mercy in Motion*

*Living the Sacraments: Finding God at the
Intersection of Heaven and Earth*

CONTENTS

Acknowledgments vii

Introduction: Loosening the Soil of Compacted Hearts
and Minds ix

Chapter 1 Proclaim a Better Way: An Alternative to Brokenness 1

Chapter 2 Introduce Jesus Christ as a Trusted Savior 13

Chapter 3 Tell of Jesus' Mighty Deeds—Past and Present.................... 25

Chapter 4 Introduce the Key to New Life: Laying Down
One's Life.. 39

Chapter 5 Proclaim the Resurrection as the Cause of Our Joy 53

Chapter 6 Extend Invitations to Follow Jesus More Closely 65

Chapter 7 Aim for the Heart.. 77

Chapter 8 Build and Deepen Commitment to a Better
Way of Living 91

Chapter 9 Equip and Empower the Next Generation
of Evangelists 107

Bibliography...125

ACKNOWLEDGMENTS

I would like to thank the following people: Leighton Drake for once again providing such excellent and engaging cartoons to enhance this book; Joe Durepos for putting the wheels in motion for this book right before riding off into the sunset (retirement); Carrie Freyer for convincing me to make this book part of the "Toolbox" family; Maria Cuadrado for shepherding the manuscript through the approval process; Vinita Hampton Wright for once again providing exquisite editing; Meghan Murphy-Gill for copy editing; and Donna Antkowiak for the beautiful design of this book.

When soil gets compacted, seeds cannot take root. Unless the soil is loosened, air, water, and nutrients cannot penetrate, and those seeds that do germinate cannot break through the surface of the soil.

So That God's Word May Penetrate

In a similar way, the seeds of God's word cannot take root in hearts that have been hardened. In today's increasingly secular world, hearts and minds have grown compacted and much more difficult to penetrate. As a result, much of our work in faith formation is like the seed that was thrown on rocky ground: it is unable to take root (Matthew 13:5–6).

If we want the seeds of God's word to take root, we need to prepare the soil of people's hearts and minds so that God's word may penetrate, obstacles that compete for nutrition may be removed, and faith may take root, break through the surface, and grow, transforming the world. Too many of our faith formation efforts go into finding ways to either throw more seed or to find bigger, better seeds to throw, when what we really need to do is prepare the soil.

> **Too many of our efforts in faith formation go into finding ways to either throw more seed or find bigger, better seeds to throw, when what we really need to be doing is preparing the soil.**

What's Changed?

Despite alarmingly dwindling numbers of people adhering to the Catholic faith, we, as a church, continue—for the most part—to sow God's word pretty much as we have done since the previous century when the soil we were

"Seems you were right about the hard soil"

sowing in was vastly different from the soil we tread upon today. In bygone days, it sufficed (or at least we thought it did) to focus our efforts almost exclusively on teaching children by relying on an academic approach (emphasizing doctrinal orthodoxy) once a week for 60–90 minutes in a parish religious education program or daily for 30–45 minutes in a Catholic school. Today, we continue to rely on a model of faith formation that served the church well 50–75 years ago but is now woefully inadequate and ill-equipped to form disciples of Jesus Christ in a rapidly changing and complex world that, more and more, considers itself to be post-Christian and no longer receptive to Christian thought.

> Today, we continue to rely on a model of faith formation that served the Church well 50–75 years ago but is now woefully inadequate and ill-equipped to form disciples of Jesus Christ.

Back in the Day

The traditional approach to sowing the seeds of faith worked well in the environment of a previous era in which the soil had the following attributes:

> People tended to live in predominantly homogenous communities and, for the most part, shared the same values and traditions.

> One parent (usually the mother and often a grandparent) stayed at home and assumed the responsibility of imparting to the children, not only Catholic values, but also devotions, practices, and traditions.

> The flow of information (and therefore, conflicting values) into the home was easily controlled before the advent of cable TV, the Internet, and social media

> respect for authority—including the clergy and hierarchy of the Church—was pervasive and unquestioned.

> The U.S. public school system tended to mirror Christian (albeit Protestant) values.

> Going to church on Sunday had little to no "competition."

In his book *Will Our Children Have Faith?* author John Westerhoff explains that an "ecology of institutions" [see sidebar]—an ecosystem, so to speak—supported the practice of the Christian faith. Soil, of course, is an ecosystem: a physical environment containing a complex network of organisms. The soil of the 21st century no longer includes the organisms (institutions) that once provided a sustainable environment for God's Word. As a result, hearts that once were open to faith have become compacted, and the soil needs to be loosened up—prepared—if it is going to once again become an environment that can sustain the living word of God. If that's going to happen, we're going to need some new strategies for doing faith formation.

"The minute you walk outside of your church on Sunday, you're in mission territory."
—Bishop Robert Barron

People Need Signs

So, when it comes to tackling this notion of preparing the soil, where do we begin? I'd like to lay the foundation for our discussion by comparing the challenge we face today with a challenge someone faced a hundred years ago. This someone—Claude C. Hopkins—discovered an approach to more effectively market a product, Pepsodent toothpaste, to an audience that, until that time, was simply not receptive to the notion of brushing one's teeth. Mr. Hopkins's approach involved adding an ingredient to Pepsodent toothpaste that made one's tongue tingle and provided a minty-fresh taste. The ingredient did nothing to prevent cavities, but it did create a trigger: it provided people with a sensation indicating that something was happening when they brushed their teeth; they could feel, taste, and smell a tangible result and experience a "reward" for brushing their teeth. Experts in marketing know that consumers appreciate (and, in fact, demand) "some kind of a signal that a product is working" (Tracy Sinclair). Mr. Hopkins's approach was so effective that it explains why, a hundred years later, brushing our teeth is a daily routine for most people.

A few millennia before Hopkins appeared on the scene, Jesus of Nazareth and then his followers, known as "the Way," understood this concept of people needing concrete evidence that what they were being invited to consider would

How'd They Do That?

The disciples understood that people needed to see a sign of the transformation that the Holy Spirit brought about in them. The reason that 3000 people joined their ranks on that first Pentecost was because those people saw that the disciples had discovered a better way of living. The disciples should have been afraid but were not; they should have been sad but were not. Their words, actions, and attitudes were triggers for those desiring a better way.

be a worthwhile and, indeed, necessary investment. People need signs. Jesus himself insisted, "No one lights a lamp and puts it in a place where it will be hidden, or under a bowl. Instead they put it on its stand, so that those who come in may see the light." (Luke 11:33). Jesus performed signs for people to see. When John the Baptist questioned whether Jesus was "the one," Jesus replied, "Go back and report to John what you hear and see: the blind receive sight, the lame walk, those who have leprosy are cleansed, the deaf hear, the dead are raised, and the good news is proclaimed to the poor." (Matthew 11:4–5).

> The *kerygma* is a simple, basic, bold, inspiring proclamation designed to invite people to consider embracing a better way of living.

An Evangelizing Message

The disciples' proclamation of an alternative reality to people who did not yet know Jesus Christ is referred to as the *kerygma*, a Greek word that means "preaching." The *kerygma* is a simple, basic, bold, and inspiring proclamation and offer of God's grace that invites people to consider a better way of living through a relationship with the risen Christ. It is an evangelizing message: a message designed to bring about conversion. Where can we see this strategy being used effectively today? Unfortunately, not so much in the church as in the secular world. Thanks to Claude C. Hopkins, this strategy is utilized regularly in the marketing world, most specifically, through TV commercials that continually promise us a better way to live.

To illustrate how formulaic this strategy is, permit me to try to sell you on an imaginary product designed specifically for catechists such as yourself. Pay close attention to the following script, and then I'll tell you how it is *kerygmatic*.

Attention catechists! Are you tired of feeling like your lessons are falling flat? Do you struggle with a nagging sense that you are not getting through to your students? Are you tired and worn out by students who just don't seem interested? If so, you need to try brand new Catechetic-O's!

Hi, I'm Joe Paprocki, author of the best-selling book, *The Catechist's Toolbox*, and the long-running blog, *The Catechist's Journey*. I've been in the catechetical ministry for over four decades, and I know what you're going through. That's why I invented Catechetic-O's, a high-energy cereal made just for catechists and loaded with the essential ingredients you need to be creative, innovative, and engaging as a catechist. After just a week of eating Catechetic-O's, I guarantee that you'll develop the capacity to plan and implement faith-formation sessions that will have your students wondering if you're the reincarnation of one of the doctors of the church!

How are Catechetic-O's different from other cereals? It's the only cereal that includes a secret ingredient I developed called Evangelate, which is like having fifty mini catechists in your head helping to stimulate creativity and innovation that even the most seasoned catechist could only hope for. So put an end to the boring sessions that are tragically causing young people to disappear from the church in alarming numbers after confirmation. Buy your first box of Catechetic-O's now for only $9.99 and watch as disciples begin popping up all around you!

But wait! There's more! Order in the next fifteen minutes and get a free bottle of Liquid Catechetic-O's for those times when you need an extra boost for important lessons such as sacramental preparation.

Your students deserve a catechist who is on fire! All it takes is one bowl a day. Join the growing army of satisfied catechists who are powered by Catechetic-O's and unleash your inner Charles Borromeo! To order your first box of Catechetic-O's, call the number on your screen or visit www.catecheticos.com. You won't be disappointed, and before long, you'll be telling other catechists to get with the Catechetic-O's program! Don't delay another moment!

Nine Strategies to "Lure You"

Now, before you wander off and try searching for the Catechetic-O's website (which does not exist), let me point out to you nine marketing strategies that can be found in this script that are formulaic in TV ads and that seek to lure potential customers to a "better way" of living.

- ➕ Point out that potential customers' current "way" is broken or unsatisfactory, needs to be repaired, fixed, or replaced, and here's the solution. ("Are you tired of . . . ?" "Well, now there's . . .")

> **Tell others about the truth that sets you free.**
> —Pope Benedict XVI

- ➕ Assure that this message/invitation is coming from a trusted source. ("Hi, I'm . . .")
- ➕ Promise and demonstrate amazing things that this "better way" offers. ("It can do the following . . .")
- ➕ Make a claim about this better way that that is so incredible that it defies logic. ("It can even . . .")
- ➕ Promise that the story gets even better ("But wait, there's more!")
- ➕ Invite potential customers to this better way of living. ("Don't be left out.")
- ➕ Aim for the heart and provoke emotions that will lead to a change of heart. ("Stop the heartache of . . .")
- ➕ Promise that potential customers' lives will never be the same but that they'll need to commit to this better way. ("In just 30 minutes a day . . .")
- ➕ Claim that potential customers will be so satisfied, they'll feel compelled to persuade others to embrace this better way. ("Soon, you'll be telling your neighbors . . .")

Why do marketers and advertisers follow these nine formulaic strategies? Because they work! After 30, 60, or 90 seconds of an advertisement that follows this formula, varying numbers of people become predisposed to purchasing the product or service advertised while numerous others become interested enough to file the information away in their heads (or their online shopping cart) for later consideration. The reason that so many people pick up the phone or go online and order products, resources, and services after viewing a commercial about them is that, like the *kerygma*, the strategy is effective: it is a simple, basic, bold, inspiring proclamation designed to invite people to consider embracing a better way of living made possible solely by the product or service being promoted. It is an "evangelizing" strategy: designed to convert people (that is, change their thinking and behavior) so that they will purchase the product or resource in question.

> **Like it or not, the business world and many other entities in the secular world are evangelizing, and we are in competition with them for hearts and minds.**

In church-talk, we use the term *pre-evangelization* to describe the work that needs to be done *prior* to full-blown evangelization and catechesis. Unfortunately, in our eagerness to evangelize and catechize as a church, we have often forgotten to pre-evangelize.

Simply put, pre-evangelization is the work of preparing people (predisposing them) to receive the Good News of Jesus Christ. Pastoral minister and author Matt Halbach writes, "an evangelization process that begins with an initial proclamation of the gospel risks sowing the seed of God's word in untilled soil, which places the quality of the conversion in jeopardy.

Hey, That's *Our* Word!

If you think I'm exaggerating or stretching the metaphor, ask yourself why there is a book available in the business section of Amazon.com—a book that has nothing to do with religion—titled *Creating Customer Evangelists*. Like it or not, the business world and many other entities in the secular world are evangelizing, and we are in competition with them for hearts and minds. Keep in mind, however, that I am not advocating that we become slick, fast-taking salespeople in imitation of TV commercials. I'm pointing out that modern marketing efforts employ a strategy that was utilized effectively by the early church to invite people to join the Way and that we need to reclaim our evangelizing mojo.

In other words, before the Good News is proclaimed, time is needed to prepare others to fully receive its message" ("New Pope, New Evangelization, New Return to Old (but Good) Ideas," *Catechetical Leader*, September 2013). Pre-evangelization is focused, not so much on catechetical instruction but rather on forging a connection, awakening desire, sparking interest, inspiring imagination, and removing obstacles, all while avoiding church jargon. Pre-evangelization draws attention to issues related to basic human needs such as security, love, and acceptance as well as people's own desires for goodness, hope, love, truth, beauty, meaning, and purpose. The goal is to establish a relationship of trust and to lay the foundation for the proclamation of the gospel and eventual formal catechetical instruction.

We can learn a thing or two about pre-evangelization from the world of marketing, which recognizes the reality of what they refer to as "the customer journey." Marketers know that while some buying is done on impulse, customers take their time when it comes to major investments and need to do their homework. In response, marketers have developed a tool known as "the marketing funnel" to take people where they are on their journey. This funnel typically consists of four steps, which in many ways correspond to the four stages of the Rite of Christian Initiation for Adults (RCIA): inquiry (doing a search), catechumenate (placing something in your "cart" but not yet ready to proceed to "checkout"), purification and enlightenment (completing the purchase), and mystagogy (returning for more information and tips, added value, and posting comments and customer feedback for the benefit of others). Let's take a closer look at these four steps.

➕ **Awareness.** Because this customer journey begins with searching, the first strategy of the marketing funnel is to raise *awareness* of two things: the consumer's needs and the seller's solution to those needs. The goal of this first step is to educate the potential customer, show the value of your product or service, and establish a relationship. This is the essence of pre-evangelization whereby the soil of people's hearts and minds is loosened and prepared.

➕ **Consideration.** As potential customers become more aware of available options, the second step of the marketing funnel is to invite them to *consideration* in which the goal is to deepen your relationship with them, further introduce them to your product/service, and personalize/tailor the connection between what you are offering and what the customer needs (targeting). This can be compared to the period of catechesis and evangelization that follows pre-evangelization.

➕ **Conversion.** Next, after potential customers have learned about the value and benefits of your product or service and what the cost to them will be, the third step of the marketing funnel is to invite *conversion* (there's that "religious" vocabulary again) in which the customer makes a decision about purchasing. In the RCIA, this decision to commit to Jesus is finalized during the period of purification and enlightenment (Lent) and ritualized with the Sacraments of Initiation at the Easter Vigil (think of how sales departments sometimes ring a bell to ritualize the completion of a sale).

➕ **Loyalty/Advocacy.** Good marketers know that the customer journey should not end with the purchase; the relationship should continue. As a result, the fourth step of the marketing funnel is known as *loyalty/advocacy*. The goal here is to retain customers and instill loyalty by delighting them with ongoing helpful information and resources that will hopefully compel them to voluntarily promote your product or services and invite others to consider them. One of the reasons too many people "drop off" after receiving confirmation or completing the RCIA is because we as a church often act as though the "sale" is complete and we move on to the next batch of potential customers. An evangelizing church seeks ways to maintain, build, and strengthen the relationship with all its members by delighting them with ongoing formation: knowledge, skills, and resources to nourish their spirituality and deepen their relationship with Jesus and the church, so that they will voluntarily promote the gospel and invite others to consider discipleship, thus beginning the cycle all over again.

> **Pre-evangelization is characterized by honest, informal, non-judgmental, and non-confrontational dialogue.**

With that whole process in mind, let's return our attention to the first step: pre-evangelization, which is where we begin preparing hearts and minds. This step is characterized by honest, informal, non-judgmental, and non-confrontational dialogue rather than the presentation of formal doctrine. A good example of this was brought to my attention by a priest friend who said that for years he had begun his marriage preparation sessions by asking the couple why they wanted to be married in the church. He eventually realized that this question immediately put the couples on edge as they sought the right answer that would permit the process to move forward. The priest changed his approach and now begins sessions by asking the couples to share how they met and fell in love. The first approach was focused on what the church wants, needs, expects, and requires. The second approach, which is focused on the couple and their story, resulted in the establishment of trust, a feeling of affirmation, and the beginnings of a relationship with the church. He initiated a spiritual conversation—one that fostered trust and a sense of security and respect. Within a context such as this, it becomes natural and less threatening for a pastoral minister to eventually invite participants to pray with him or her and to invite them to share intercessions (pray for the needs of others). The goal of pre-evangelization is to lay the foundation for moving to a deeper and more formal exploration of the Catholic faith, but that can't happen unless hearts and minds have been prepared.

Prompting Spiritual Conversations

Spiritual conversations can be prompted by questions such as the following:

1. Who has been an inspiration in your life?
2. What have been the milestones in your life?
3. What do you like or enjoy most about what you do?
4. Who or what has shaped you into the person you are today?
5. What lessons have you learned as a result of . . . ?
6. What makes you happy?
7. What dreams do you still wish to pursue?

Eventually such questions can become more God-centered, such as:

1. How would you describe your relationship with God right now?
2. What obstacles are standing in the way of you growing closer to God?
3. Who is your favorite saint?
4. What is your favorite Gospel story?

An elderly and curmudgeonly pastor reluctantly attended an evangelization workshop to seek out strategies for stemming the rising tide of young families who were no longer attending Sunday Mass. Of all the strategies, he selected one that involved visiting former parishioners' homes for dinner, thinking, *At least I'll get a good meal out of the experience.* When the pastor arrived at the home of one family, the parents invited him to sit in the living room with their young son while they prepared the meal in the kitchen. Not sure of how to make conversation with the young boy, the pastor asked him what they were having for dinner. The boy replied, "Goat." "Goat?" replied the startled pastor. "Are you sure about that?" "Yes," said the boy. "When my parents were getting ready for work this morning, my mom told my dad, 'Remember, we're having the old goat for dinner tonight.'"

Becoming Evangelizing Catechists

As we forge ahead in this book, I am going to explore these nine strategies from the *kerygma*—the disciples' first proclamation of the Way to people who had not yet encountered Christ—that we catechists can and must use in our faith formation to be more evangelizing catechists who know how to prepare hearts and minds! Just as consumers need some kind of signal that a product is working, those we teach need some kind of signal that following Jesus is a better way to live.

Join me as we look at these nine strategies that are at the heart of the amazingly effective *kerygma*—the first proclamation of the Good News of salvation by the disciples that effectively "prepared the soil" and predisposed hearts and minds to accept the gospel message and laid the foundation for more than 2,000 years of Christianity:

1. Strategy #1. Point out that potential believers' current "way" is broken or unsatisfactory and needs to be repaired or replaced. (*We begin by drawing attention to our human brokenness and we proclaim a better way to be human: an alternative known as the reign of God.*)

2. Strategy #2. Assure that this message and invitation is coming from a trusted source. (*We offer assurance that Jesus Christ, the Son of God, is our Savior and that he and his disciples—the church—can be trusted.*)

3. Strategy #3. Promise and demonstrate amazing things that this "better way" offers. (*We tell the stories of Jesus healing the sick, opening the eyes of the blind, calming the storms, walking on water, and changing our own lives.*)

4. Strategy #4. Make a claim about this better way that that is so incredible that it defies logic. (*We explain that Jesus died for us so that we might have eternal life.*)

5. Strategy #5. Promise that the story gets even better (but wait, there's more!). (*We proclaim that Jesus Christ rose from the dead and lives and remains with us.*)

6. Strategy #6. Invite potential believers to this better way of living. (*We extend an invitation to have your life transformed by following this better way of Jesus.*)

7. Strategy #7. Aim for the heart and provoke emotions that will lead to a change of heart. (*We call people to repentance: a letting go of old ways in order to embrace a better way.*)

8. Strategy #8. Promise that potential believers' lives will never be the same, but that they will need to commit to this better way of living. (*Offer opportunities for ongoing deepening of this relationship with Jesus Christ.*)

9. Strategy #9. Claim that potential believers will be so satisfied, they'll feel compelled to persuade others to embrace this better way. (*Empower others to go forth to share this better way with others.*)

Today more than ever, the world needs to see evidence that there is a "better way"—a different way of being human that is not guided by the bankrupt values and philosophies of a broken world but by the life-giving message of selfless and redeeming love proclaimed by Jesus Christ. This is the quest of the evangelizing catechist: to provide convincing evidence that there is indeed a better way—the way of Jesus Christ—which surpasses all other ways. And these nine strategies effectively "prepare the soil" so that hearts and minds can become more receptive to the Good News of Jesus Christ.

> **Today more than ever, the world needs to see evidence that there is a "better way."**

Before We Go Any Further, a Little Fervorino

Proclaiming the gospel has never been easy. And it seems to be getting harder. I'm sure you'll agree with me that, in recent times, it has become overwhelmingly difficult to proclaim the Good News of Jesus Christ given the seemingly irreparable damage the Roman Catholic Church has sustained as a result of the clergy sex-abuse scandal and cover-up by church leaders. And yet in my travels across the country, I continue to come across countless numbers of catechists and pastoral ministers like yourself who remain fiercely undaunted when it comes to the task of fulfilling our baptismal call to proclaim the gospel message to others in word and in deed. Are we disillusioned? At times. Are we saddened? Yes. Are we angry? Oh, hell yes! Are we giving up? Oh, hell no! We know that, while the church has been damaged, Jesus and his life-giving message are invulnerable. And we fully intend to continue proclaiming that Good News to all who seek a better way.

To do that, however, we are going to need to loosen the compacted soil of hearts and minds to predispose people to be receptive to God's word. For the past few decades, I have had the privilege of journeying with an army of no fewer than a half-million catechists, as we have attempted to become more effective at proclaiming the gospel. During that time, I have never seen challenges as great as the ones we face today—challenges that have convinced many people to close their minds and hearts to the message of Christianity. Farmers and gardeners know that compacted soil can be returned to good health but not without some serious tilling! I am convinced that, with the help and guidance of the Holy Spirit, we can effectively prepare the soil of hearts and minds to create a fertile environment for the planting of the seeds of God's word. We do so, "hard pressed on every side, but not crushed; perplexed, but not in despair; persecuted, but not abandoned; struck down, but not destroyed" (2 Corinthians 4:8–9). The Good News is that sin and death do *not* have the last word. Our institutional church may be broken, but the Spirit of our Lord Jesus Christ—a Spirit of love, joy, peace, patience, kindness, goodness, faithfulness, gentleness, and self-control—prevails. From death comes new life. And you and I are called to give witness to that to the ends of the earth. Let's get to work preparing the soil in the fields of the Lord!

> Let's get to work preparing the soil in the fields of the Lord!

Questions for Reflection and Discussion

> What, in your mind, has caused the "soil" of people's hearts and minds to become "compacted" or less receptive to practicing faith than in times past?

> What is your understanding of *pre-evangelization*? How is it different from evangelization per se?

> What changes in the "soil" of society and culture have made it more difficult to sow the seeds of faith today?

> What is your understanding of the *kerygma*? What does it mean to say that our faith-formation efforts today must be more *kerygmatic*?

> When were you persuaded by an advertisement or a TV commercial to make a purchase? What specifically persuaded you to do so?

> What does it mean to say that the business world is "evangelizing" more effectively than the church is?

> Of the nine *kerygma* strategies (see pg. xx), which one strikes you as most urgently needed? Which one do you personally need to improve?

Scripture

But the seed falling on good soil refers to someone who hears the word and understands it. This is the one who produces a crop, yielding a hundred, sixty or thirty times what was sown. MATTHEW 13:23

Prayer

Loving God, prepare the soil of my heart that I may become more receptive to your sowing of the Word in my life. Help me, in turn, to prepare the soil of people's hearts so that your Word may take root and yield a bountiful harvest. Amen.

Chapter 1

Proclaim a Better Way: An Alternative to Brokenness

Have you ever noticed how many advertisements begin with, "Are you tired of . . . ?" The not-so-subtle message is that something is missing from your life or that something in your life, as you live it now, is broken and needs repair. For example, an ad for a flu remedy will go out of its way to illustrate just how miserable it is to have the flu—something that resonates with anyone who has endured this misfortune.

Creating a Sense of Need

Often, these TV commercial depictions of what is broken or missing from our lives are exaggerated to the point of being comical. Ads for new kitchen gadgets show frustrated cooks in the kitchen floundering about with ineffective utensils that take too long, don't slice well, require too much effort, or create a catastrophic mess. If you are the unlucky owner of such obsolete utensils, the message is clear: Your life is miserable. After pointing out this misery, however, the ad quickly announces that it is offering a solution, a new product that will solve all your problems and make all these headaches disappear. In essence, they promise a better way of living.

Remember, the first step in marketing is to respond to those who are searching by raising awareness about two things: customers' needs and

"I've decided to start reading a much better story."

the "solution" a product or service offers. This step involves creating an urgent sense of need. Likewise, the first step in preparing hearts and minds and in being a more evangelizing catechist is to invite those you are teaching to recognize that something is missing from their lives or that the lives they are living are broken, in need of repair, or at least unfulfilled.

The first step in marketing is to create an urgent sense of need.

As the Apostles did, we must proclaim that our current reality is broken (and that we are the unfortunate heirs of that brokenness) and that God has intervened through his only Son, Jesus Christ, to offer us an alternative known as the reign of God: a better way of living and being human.

Bad News, Good News

In a homiletics course I once took, the professor wisely suggested that every homily should begin with "bad news" and proceed to the "Good News" of Jesus Christ. He referred to how comedians often do "good news/bad news" jokes such as this: A doctor calls his patient and says, "I have good news and bad news. I got your test results back and you have only 24 hours to live!" The patient responds, "That's terrible, doctor, what's the good news?" The doctor responds, "Actually, that was the good news. The bad news is, I was supposed to call you 24 hours ago!"

Feeling Others' Pain

Proclaiming brokenness is NOT to proclaim doom, to act as "Debbie downers," to make people feel miserable or guilty about their present state of life, or, worst of all, to point fingers at people and tell them that they are worthless sinners and must repent. In ages past, this "hellfire and brimstone" approach to evangelization may have been moderately effective in frightening people into changing their lives for fear that they might face an eternity in the fires of hell. In today's more sophisticated world, such an approach simply will not work. Instead, we who minister in the name of Jesus need to pastorally empathize with the hurt, pain, or emptiness that people—including ourselves—are carrying around in one form or another.

The professor went on to explain that, in a homily (and for our purposes, in faith formation), we reverse the "good news/bad news" formula and rely on a "bad news/good news" approach. We begin by inviting our listeners/learners to consider some aspect of their reality that is broken—something that resonates with people so that as they listen to us, they are thinking, *Yeah, that's the story of my life!*

> **Before we proclaim the Good News, we need to identify the reasons they need to hear it.**

Before we proclaim the Good News, we need to convince people that they need to hear it, and we do that by helping them get in touch with their own incompleteness, emptiness, and/or brokenness. We need to explain how we humans are prone to dysfunctional behavior and cannot save ourselves from such dysfunctions but need an intervention that sets us on the road to recovery.

Changing Our Narrative

The truth is, too many of us are walking around with narratives that are unhealthy, unfulfilling, and, dare I say, dangerous to our own well-being and the well-being of others. Some of these narratives tell us that we are . . .

worthless	unlovable	uninteresting
ugly	shameful	undeserving
fat	inferior	incapable of happiness
unreliable	untalented	

Still other narratives tell us that in order to be happy, we need . . .

money	pleasure	conquest
power	control	prestige
possessions/success	popularity	fame

The School of Hard Knocks

Many people carry a damaged view of their story and themselves because they have suffered some hard knocks. At any given time, any gathering of humans will include varying percentages of people suffering from unemployment, chronic pain, divorce, depression, broken relationships, economic woes, domestic abuse, stress of caretaking, thoughts of suicide, loss of a loved one, sexual abuse, anxiety, loneliness, chronic disease, bullying, and poor self-image, just to name a few.

The Good News of Jesus Christ is that these false, misleading, damaged, and broken narratives can and must be changed! Jesus proclaims a different story about a new reality called the reign of God in which we are

To evangelize is to invite people to "change their minds" and reject false narratives in place of the saving narrative of Jesus Christ.

➕ rescued (from sin)

➕ restored (to our intimate relationship with the Father) and

➕ reassured (by a loving God who provides us with everything we need and is with us always). Jesus' proclamation of the Gospel begins with the word, "Repent!" which means to "change your mind." To evangelize is to invite people to change their minds and reject false narratives in place of the saving narrative of Jesus Christ. Evangelization invites people to recognize how compacted our collective hearts and minds have become and to till the soil of their own lives in order to be capable of imagining new possibilities.

That Art of Changing Minds

How do we go about catechizing to facilitate repentance—the changing of minds? What might this look like in a catechetical setting? To illustrate, I'm going to look (at the time this was written) to the Gospel for the upcoming Sunday, the Second Sunday of Lent, which is the story of the Transfiguration (Mark 9:2–10).

1. I begin by reading and reflecting on the Scripture passage, asking myself, What is the Good News of this story? (It may be helpful to look at some commentaries). Know that there is not just one correct answer to this question, "What is the Good News of this story?"

   After six days Jesus took Peter, James and John with him and led them up a high mountain, where they were all alone. There he was transfigured before them. His clothes became dazzling white, whiter than anyone in the world could bleach them. And there appeared before them Elijah and Moses, who were talking with Jesus. Peter said to Jesus, "Rabbi, it is good for us to be here. Let us put up three shelters—one for you, one for Moses and one for Elijah." (He did not know what to say, they were so frightened.) Then a cloud appeared and covered them, and a voice came from the cloud: "This is my Son, whom I love. Listen to him!" Suddenly, when they looked around, they no longer saw anyone with them except Jesus. As they were coming down the mountain, Jesus gave them orders not to tell anyone what they had seen until the Son of Man had risen from the dead. They kept the matter to themselves, discussing what "rising from the dead" meant.

2. In my reflection, I am led to focus on the phrase, "This is my Son, whom I love. Listen to him!" (Mark 9:7).

3. In my mind, then, the good news of this story is that we have access to the voice of God through Jesus Christ, who is truly God from God, Light from Light!

4. The bad news, then, is that we live in a time of confusion and "alternative facts." We often don't know who to listen to. We find ourselves lost, confused, and even in despair, not knowing where truth can be found.

For my lesson, I would simply reverse the order of the above and start by inviting my learners to recognize that when we turn on the TV or explore social media, we are bombarded by so many voices claiming to speak the truth that it can make our heads spin! For younger children who may not be as aware of current events in the news, I would invite them to recognize that they hear a lot of mixed messages from their friends about what is right and what is wrong and that it creates a lot of stress and confusion for the them. Then, I would announce the good news: "In today's gospel, however, we have good news! We learn that the voice of Jesus is the voice of God and therefore can be trusted. It is a voice that cuts through all the confusion and shows us the way. It is a voice that we *need*. It is to our benefit to 'Listen to Him' rather than to the many voices that steer us down the wrong path." This session, then, is designed to bring about repentance: a change of mind about whose voice we should be listening to in order to overcome our brokenness.

> **Fruitfulness comes out of brokenness.**
> —HENRI NOUWEN

Throughout the year, Father Don preaches inspiring homilies at Sunday Mass, urging his congregation to become an army of ministers reaching out to people who are experiencing brokenness. He even created different "branches" of his army for people to serve in: one branch served those who were homeless, another served those with chronic illness, another served those who experienced the loss of a loved one, and so on. One Sunday after Mass, inspired parishioners were lining up as usual to join the various branches of "Father Don's Army" when he noticed one young man quickly dashing to his car in the parking lot. He caught up with him and asked him why he was in such a hurry to leave and why he didn't want to join "Father Don's Army." The young man said, "Oh, I'm already a member of your army Father." Father Don replied, "I hate to say it, but I don't recall seeing you here before except maybe on Christmas and Easter. What branch of my army do you belong to?" The young man replied, "Secret Service."

Brokenness: The Key to Salvation

It is no coincidence that we begin our celebration of the Mass with the Penitential Act in which we acknowledge our brokenness.

> I confess to almighty God
>   and to you, my brothers and sisters,
> that I have greatly sinned,
>   in my thoughts and in my words,
> in what I have done and
>   in what I have failed to do,
>
> [Pray while striking the breast three times.]
> through my fault, through my fault,
>   through my most grievous fault;
> (*The Roman Missal*)

It is this very brokenness that is the key to our salvation, for, without acknowledging our

Without acknowledging our brokenness, we remain unreceptive to God's grace: the soil of our hearts and minds remains compacted.

brokenness, we remain unreceptive to God's grace: the soil of our hearts and minds remains compacted.

Light Comes Through the Cracks

When we embrace our brokenness, we become vulnerable, and it is through the very "cracks" in our being that the grace of God can and will enter.

As followers of Jesus, we are called to let our light shine before all. However, it is crucial to remember that this light is coming from beyond ourselves and can only shine before all if it can get through the cracks in our being. Once it does, it floods through and becomes visible to all. This is precisely why Jesus went after the Pharisees and what he called their self-righteousness. Jesus tells the parable of the Pharisee and the tax collector in which the two men go up to the Temple to pray.

> The Pharisee stood by himself and prayed: "God, I thank you that I am not like other people—robbers, evildoers, adulterers—or even like this tax collector. I fast twice a week and give a tenth of all I get." But the tax collector stood at a distance. He would not even look up to heaven, but beat his breast and said, "God, have mercy on me, a sinner." I tell you that this man, rather than the other, went home justified before God. For all those who exalt themselves will be humbled, and those who humble themselves will be exalted. (Luke 18:11–14)

The reason Jesus insisted that sinners are closer to the Reign of God than the Pharisees is precisely because many sinners are painfully aware of their brokenness and are not deluded by any sense of self-righteousness which is a refusal of God's grace. Just as the Mass begins with our admission of brokenness (notice how, in the Penitential Act mentioned above that we are directed to strike our breast in imitation of the tax collector), our role as catechists is to invite and enable those we teach to recognize and embrace their brokenness and shed any delusion of self-sufficiency, as the first step toward salvation. We must convince others that the message we are sharing—the Good News—is not just something nice—it is something we all need. To proceed otherwise is to ignore the very reality of the human condition: to be human is to be imperfect.

> **Our role as catechists is to invite and enable those we teach to recognize and embrace their brokenness.**

The Good News as an Antidote to Brokenness

Here I offer the following examples of doctrinal topics followed by the "bad news" for which they are antidotes. Remember, each of these doctrinal topics is *multivalent*, which means that there are numerous ways of interpreting the Good News it proclaims and the bad news it dispels. These are simply examples.

⊕ **Doctrinal Topic:** The Beatitudes
Point of Pain/Bad News: Our world seems hopelessly driven by destructive attitudes of selfishness, greed, power, and violence.
Good News/Antidote: Jesus Christ proclaims an alternative way of thinking and acting that subverts the status quo and leads to a transformed reality.

⊕ **Doctrinal Topic:** The Ten Commandments
Point of Pain/Bad News: There are so many conflicting voices claiming to speak the truth that it can be very confusing to know what it right and what is wrong.
Good News/Antidote: God provides a clear roadmap for how to live according to his will and to experience fullness of life by loving God and others.

⊕ **Doctrinal Topic:** The Real Presence
Point of Pain/Bad News: We often feel abandoned and alone, as though God were very distant from us or not present at all.
Good News/Antidote: In and through the Eucharist, Jesus Christ—the Son of God—is physically present to us. We are not alone.

⊕ **Doctrinal Topic:** Reconciliation
Point of Pain/Bad News: We are flawed and prone to thinking and acting in ways that can be hurtful to ourselves and others, and we seem powerless to overcome this tendency.
Good News/Antidote: Through Jesus Christ, our sins are forgiven, and we are restored to full relationship with the Father.

⊕ **Doctrinal Topic:** The Fruits of the Spirit
Point of Pain/Bad News: Our world is filled with such turmoil and confusion that it often seems impossible to see God's presence.
Good News/Antidote: Whenever we see the traits of love, joy, peace, (the Fruits of the Spirit) on display, we know that God is present.

➕ **Doctrinal Topic:** The Trinity
Point of Pain/Bad News: We often experience isolation, loneliness, and lack of community.
Good News/Antidote: We are made in the image and likeness of the triune God, whose very identity is communal.

➕ **Doctrinal Topic:** Sin
Point of Pain/Bad News: Sin (evil) often appears to have the upper hand in our world, and living a good life seems impossible.
Good News/Antidote: Through his Cross and Resurrection, Jesus Christ has defeated sin once and for all, filling us with confident hope in the face of evil.

Doing Theological Reflection

You can reverse this dynamic and begin by identifying common points of pain or examples of bad news in our world and in the lives of those you teach. Then reflect on experience and the faith Tradition that leads to an aspect of the gospel and church teaching that serves as an antidote. Try your hand at it using the examples below. Remember, there is no single correct answer; this is simply an exercise to develop the skill of connecting faith and life. I completed the first one for you as an example.

> The wound is the place where the Light enters you.
> —Rumi

➕ **Point of Pain/Bad News:** Despair
Good News/Antidote: Hope
Related Doctrinal Concept: The Resurrection

➕ **Point of Pain/Bad News:** Anxiety
Good News/Antidote: _____
Related Doctrinal Concept: _____

➕ **Point of Pain/Bad News:** Deceit/Dishonesty
Good News/Antidote: _____
Related Doctrinal Concept: _____

➕ **Point of Pain/Bad News:** Materialism/Possessions
   Good News/Antidote: _____
   Related Doctrinal Concept: _____

➕ **Point of Pain/Bad News:** Broken Relationships
   Good News/Antidote: _____
   Related Doctrinal Concept: _____

➕ **Point of Pain/Bad News:** Failure
   Good News/Antidote: _____
   Related Doctrinal Concept: _____

➕ **Point of Pain/Bad News:** Economic Hardship
   Good News/Antidote: _____
   Related Doctrinal Concept: _____

I highly recommend that as you prepare any and all your lessons as a catechist you identify the good news you are proclaiming and the bad news that message is dispelling. Look to current events as examples to illustrate the bad news that surrounds us but that can and will be overcome by the Good News of Jesus Christ!

True Tales

Here's an example of a time when I taught a lesson and effectively began by introducing bad news and then used that to segue to the good news of the lesson.

The theme of the lesson was on the Beatitudes as a recipe for true happiness, and it was for an eighth-grade class. As it turns out, at the time I was preparing to teach this lesson, there was a high-profile celebrity death in the news: actor Philip Seymour Hoffman had tragically overdosed on drugs. I began the session by bringing this to their attention and asking how many were aware of it (most were). I talked about how sad it was that someone with so much talent and with seemingly everything going for him (fame and fortune and a successful career) felt the need to take drugs.

I asked the young people—somewhat rhetorically—why they thought someone

> While the world offers us all kinds of things that are supposed to make us happy, many of them are fleeting, misleading, or downright dangerous and disastrous.

would feel the need to take drugs even though they seemed to have everything that could make someone happy. The young people grappled with that and, as expected, had a difficult time answering it but agreed that it was sad and tragic. One young person, however, insisted that it was stupid for someone who had so much to seek happiness through drugs. This gave me the opportunity to say, "That may be so, but it is true that many of us who have so much are still not happy, and many people—young and old—seek to fill that empty space in our hearts through a variety of ways, such as drugs, alcohol, sex, money, possessions, power, and so on. It seems that, even though we have so much, we're still not happy."

I let that sit there for a moment just to sink in and resonate ("Yeah, that's the story of my life"). Then I said, "While the world offers us all kinds of things that are supposed to make us happy, many of them are fleeting, misleading, or downright dangerous and disastrous. Today, we're going to learn about a happiness that is lasting; a happiness that cannot be taken away from us; a happiness that truly fills the empty space within us. It's a happiness that can come only from God."

I used that, then, as the segue into our lesson that evening about the Beatitudes as a recipe for true happiness. The bad news of a celebrity drug overdose—which is illustrative of a pervasive unhappiness or restlessness that we all experience—provided an entry point into their young lives and allowed me to introduce the antidote to

> God's way is indeed the better way. And *that* is good news!

that pervasive unhappiness: a happiness offered to us by Jesus and described in the Beatitudes. Philip Seymour Hoffman's tragic story is an extreme example of what too many people experience: we fail to appreciate what we have and instead seek ways to numb the pain or fill the empty space within, not realizing that only God can fill that space and heal that pain. God's way is indeed the better way. And *that* is good news!

Questions for Reflection and Discussion

> What is one product you have purchased because you were convinced it would change your life or make your life easier? What was the bad news that this product claimed to be the antidote for?
> How can we—as catechists and evangelizers—effectively use this bad news/good news strategy to proclaim God's Word?

> What do you think are some of the most common unhealthy narratives that our culture or society tends to peddle?
> What is an unhealthy narrative that you have personally grappled with?
> How would you explain in your own words what it means to say that our Christian narrative is one of "rescue, restoration, and reassurance"? What is your personal experience of these three realities in relation to the Gospel?
> Why is self-righteousness such an obstacle to receiving God' grace?
> What are some of the most common points of pain you recognize in those you teach? How can the Good News of Jesus serve as an antidote?
> When have you overcome the "delusion of self-sufficiency" and admitted that you needed help with a problem or situation?

Scripture

The Lord is close to the brokenhearted
and saves those who are crushed in spirit.
PSALM 34:18

Prayer

Good and gracious God, help me recognize my own brokenness and turn to you for healing. Fill my heart with compassion to reach out to the brokenhearted and proclaim the good news of your nearness to them so that they might experience your healing grace. Amen.

Chapter 2

Introduce Jesus Christ as a Trusted Savior

I'm sure you are familiar with the concept of an intervention: a carefully planned gathering of trusted family and friends in which they confront a loved one about his or her addiction and offer an opportunity to get treatment. The rationale behind an intervention is that the person afflicted with an addiction is incapable of "saving" him or herself; the initiative must come from outside the individual. In essence, it is the recognition that we are incapable of healing ourselves of our own dysfunctions. For such an intervention to be successful, it must come from a trusted source.

Whom Can You Trust?

Ultimately, advertisements seek to gain your trust; the goal is to convince you that your money will be well spent on whatever product or service is being sold. As we invite people to consider embracing the gospel, we need to convince them that this invitation comes from a trusted source—Jesus Christ, the Son of God—and that we are incapable of "getting there" on our own. We need a divine intervention.

In our faith formation, we need to make it clear that, when it comes to the power of sin, we are incapable of overcoming it on our own (that's the essence of original sin), which is why God carefully planned an intervention—the Incarnation—to lovingly confront us

"Would this be a good time to talk to you about the meaning of life?"

> ## Somebody Save Me!
> We cannot overestimate the importance of presenting Jesus Christ not simply as a wise philosopher, a smart teacher, or a swell fella, but as a savior. Think of this image: You are sinking in a pool of quicksand. The last thing you need or want is for a philosopher to come by to talk about the existential ramifications of your situation. You need someone to save you. Sin is like that pool of quicksand. We are incapable of pulling ourselves out of the muck: we need a savior.

with our need to repent and accept the opportunity to enter "recovery" through Jesus Christ.

We said in the first chapter that we live in a broken world: the human family is dysfunctional. We can be lifted out from this "pool of quicksand" known as sin only by a power beyond ourselves. It is the same logic used in twelve-step programs: the first step in recovery is to admit powerlessness over the addiction (and that one's life has become unmanageable) while the second step is to believe that a power greater than oneself—a power that can be trusted—can restore one to sanity. This power greater than ourselves is God, "who so loved that world, that he gave his one and only Son, that whoever believes in him shall not perish but have eternal life." (John 3:16)

> **In our faith formation, we need to make it clear that, when it comes to the power of sin, we are incapable of overcoming it on our own.**

Jesus Is a Game Changer

So how does this manifest itself in faith formation?

First and foremost, it means that our catechesis must be Christocentric. It's all about Jesus. Our mandate is to put those we teach, "not only in touch, but also in communion and intimacy, with Jesus Christ" (*General Directory for Catechesis*, 80). We bring others into "communion and intimacy" with Jesus not only by talking *about* him, but also by inviting those we teach to encounter him through prayer. Our entire session should take place within a "climate of prayer" so that the experience resembles the Mass (worship) more than class (academics). More specifically, we need to lead those we teach in experiences of reflective prayer during which they can talk and listen to God speak to their hearts. We must not only teach prayers but, more importantly, how to pray. St. Ignatius said that prayer should resemble one friend speaking to another. It is our job as catechists to introduce those we teach to this trusted friend, Jesus Christ.

> **Our entire session should take place within a "climate of prayer" so that the experience resembles the Mass (worship) more than class (academics).**

Second, we must speak more candidly about our own relationship with Jesus Christ. As Catholics, we too often hide behind very sterile language such as, "The Church says . . ." or "The *Catechism* teaches us . . ." rather than directly mentioning the name of Jesus Christ as our trusted friend, so that those we teach understand that this is a relationship we are inviting them into. For example, "In my relationship with Jesus, I have learned . . ." I specifically encourage catechists and Catholic schoolteachers, as they introduce themselves on the first day of class, to say a little bit about why they are doing this ministry and how Jesus is an important part of their lives.

In advertising, marketers present their product or service as

- a game changer and a necessity, and;
- as coming from a trusted source.

We must do no less: Do not invite people to "sprinkle a little Jesus" into their lives to make it sweeter. Rather, proclaim Jesus as a game changer—a necessity if we hope to overcome our human dysfunction—and as a trusted source: no ordinary man, but "God from God, Light from Light, true God from true God, begotten, not made, consubstantial with the Father."

> **We proclaim Jesus as a game changer.**

Establishing Trust

Establishing trust is central to any concept of organizational development. Many experts in leadership emphasize that one of the first priorities of an effective leader is to establish a climate of trust. In other words, people need to know that they are safe in this environment that they are being invited into. This is especially crucial in a faith formation or spiritual environment where people are being invited to entrust their entire being to the Person of Jesus Christ and his church. It should come as no surprise, then, that this issue of trust has been heightened in recent years due to the egregious breach of trust that is the clergy sex abuse scandal and cover-up. At a time when trust in institutional organizations is already at an all-time low, the added damage caused by this scandal to the Catholic Church has resulted in an evaporation of the trust that people once placed in the church. For us to effectively evangelize and catechize those entrusted to us, we will need to re-establish that trust.

How do we establish a climate of trust? According to Charles H. Green, founder and CEO of Trusted Advisor Associates LLC, trust can be boiled down to the following four factors:

- Credibility: people need to trust what their leaders say
- Reliability: people need to trust what their leaders do
- Intimacy: people need to trust that they can share information with their leaders
- Self-Orientation: people need to know that their leaders are not self-absorbed but have others' best interests at heart

Helping People Feel Safe

In a much-viewed TED talk, "Why Good Leaders Make You Feel Safe," management theorist Simon Sinek emphasizes that effective leaders draw their people into a circle of trust, a place where they feel safe from the dangers surrounding them, and also are empowered to battle those forces of danger. In that talk, Sinek says, "You know, in the military, they give medals to people who are willing to sacrifice themselves so that others may gain. In business, we give bonuses to people who sacrifice others so that we may gain. We have it backwards." How true. Sinek goes on to say that, when people feel safe and secure and within a circle of trust, remarkable things can happen: "When we feel safe inside the organization, we will naturally combine our talents and our strengths and work tirelessly to face the dangers outside and seize the opportunities."

Green developed an interesting tool he calls the "Trust Equation" that can assist organizations in measuring the degree of trust that members have in leadership. The equation looks like this:

$$T = C + R + I \div S\text{-}O$$

(Trust equals Credibility plus Reliability
plus Intimacy divided by Self-Orientation)

In other words, after you rate each of the four factors on a scale from 1 to 10, the trust equation is achieved by dividing the sum of the first three factors (credibility, reliability, and intimacy) by the fourth factor, self-orientation. For example, if a leader is rated accordingly . . .

> Do not let your hearts be troubled. Trust in God; trust also in me.
> —JESUS CHRIST (JOHN 14:1)

+ credibility = 7 (I find what this leader says to be credible for the most part)

+ reliability = 5 (I find what this leader does is not always totally reliable)

+ intimacy = 4 (I really don't feel I can confide in this leader)

+ self-orientation = 8 (this leader is usually self-absorbed and gives me and others little attention)

. . . the trust equation is a mediocre 2 (7 + 5 + 4 ÷ 8 = 2).

However, if a leader receives the following rating . . .

+ credibility = 7 (I find what this leader says to be credible for the most part)

+ reliability = 7 (I find what this leader does to be usually be reliable)

+ intimacy = 7 (I feel comfortable confiding in this leader)

+ self-orientation = 2 (this leader devotes a good deal of attention to me and others instead of to him/herself)

. . . the trust equation is an impressive 10.5 (7 + 7 + 7 ÷ 2 = 10.5).

It is crucial that we, today's catechists and evangelizers, can and must establish trust. This requires us to do the following:

➕ **Speak credibly:** What we have to say must be sound and must resonate with all that is good, true, and beautiful.

➕ **Act reliably:** Our actions must flow from and match our words; they must be an authentic embodiment of what we say.

➕ **Be approachable:** Those we serve must feel comfortable and safe confiding in us.

➕ **Focus on others:** Our attention must be on those we serve, not on ourselves.

Creating a Climate of Trust

Likewise, it is our job to present Jesus Christ as someone who is credible, reliable, worthy of intimacy, and selfless, if others are to place their trust in him. We'll come back to that in a moment, but first, let's look more closely at how a leader establishes trust in a group or organization. Here are some specific skills and strategies for establishing a climate of trust that will enable participants to feel safe and secure in a group setting:

> **It is our job to present Jesus Christ as someone who is credible, reliable, worthy of intimacy, and selfless, if others are to place their trust in him.**

➕ **Clarify expected behaviors for all (including yourself).** Trust is built when participants know what behaviors are encouraged and what behaviors are unacceptable. They should even be invited to construct this list or at least add to it. Participants can also benefit from hearing you, as the leader/facilitator of the group, identify which behaviors are required of you in order to ensure a safe environment.

➕ **Consistently confront violations of unacceptable behaviors and affirm adherence.** Trust is built when participants see that the aforementioned codes of conduct are enforced and that there are consequences or repercussions for violations of such codes of conduct.

➕ **Encourage and protect expression.** Trust is built when participants feel free to express themselves and know that when they do, they will be respected and their contributions will be appreciated.

+ **Encourage and embrace candor.** Trust is built when participants are allowed the freedom to grapple with concepts being presented and to respectfully express their disagreement with impunity.

+ **Encourage risk taking and do not fear failure.** Trust is built when participants know that they can use their unique gifts and talents to try new things and that they need not fear repercussions simply for trying.

+ **Incorporate cooperative learning opportunities.** Trust is built when participants interact with one another to build trust in the group, not just between them and you, but also among themselves.

> Love cannot live
> where there is no trust.
> —EDITH HAMILTON

+ **Share responsibility.** Trust is built when participants (especially older children, youth, and adults) enjoy a sense of ownership and shared responsibility for the direction of the group.

+ **Show compassion and empathy.** Trust is built when participants know that you truly care about and understand them.

+ **Celebrate diversity.** Trust is built when participants know that their unique talents, gifts, characteristics, and identity are welcome and that they are not simply expected to conform or perform tasks.

+ **Generously affirm others.** Trust is built when participants know that they and their contributions are held in esteem and are appreciated.

+ **Admit your own mistakes, shortcomings, and limitations.** Trust is built when participants recognize your transparency and honesty, which, in turn, encourages them to be transparent.

+ **Be available.** Trust is built when participants know that you are approachable and that they can confide in you.

+ **Respect and observe boundaries.** While boundaries sound like something negative—a way of shutting out others—they can be quite positive—a means of protecting that which is sacred. In the Old Testament, we learn that the Temple in Jerusalem—the focal point of God's sacred presence among his people—had various boundaries that separated Gentiles, Jewish women, Jewish men, and the priests

A young lady was having a hard time entrusting her life to Jesus Christ. On one very stressful day, as she rushed to get to an important job interview, she was searching desperately for a parking spot in a crowded lot. Noticing that she would soon be late, she cried out in desperation, "Lord, if you find me a parking spot, I promise to entrust my entire life to you and to start going to church." The words were barely out of her mouth, when a spot opened up right in front of her car. The young lady looked up to heaven and said, "Never mind, I found one."

from the Ark of the Covenant, which "contained" God's sacred presence. In the New Testament, Jesus replaced that Temple with the temple of his own body, and St. Paul taught that we are temples of the Holy Spirit. As a result, we are called to respect the sacredness of ourselves and one another. One of the ways we do this is by observing physical, emotional, and behavioral boundaries.

Doing the work of establishing trust is not an interruption in our evangelizing/catechizing efforts; it is a prerequisite to meaningful accompaniment and a crucial step in preparing hearts and minds.

> **Doing the work of establishing trust is not an interruption in our evangelizing/catechizing efforts; it is a prerequisite to meaningful accompaniment and a crucial step in preparing hearts and minds.**

Trusting Jesus

Now, let's return to this notion of presenting Jesus Christ as someone who is credible, reliable, worthy of intimacy, and selfless—the four traits that form the basis for trust. Sometimes, when we seek to convince others of our own trustworthiness, we can go "over-the-top" in our efforts, as was depicted in a famous scene from the movie *The Blues Brothers* when Jake Blues (John Belushi) tries to convince the Mystery Woman (Carrie Fisher) that his reasons for standing her up at the altar were legitimate:

> "I ran outta gas. I had a flat tire. I didn't have enough money for cab fare. My tux didn't come back from the cleaners. An old friend came in

from outta town. Someone stole my car. There was an earthquake, a terrible flood, locusts. IT WASN'T MY FAULT! I SWEAR TO GOD!"

Despite the fact they he's clearly lying, I've always loved how Jake's voice builds in intensity until it reaches a crescendo in the words, "IT WASN'T MY FAULT! I SWEAR TO GOD!" It doesn't take much to imagine the section of the Nicene Creed that proclaims that Jesus is no ordinary person recited in a similar voice—building in intensity and reaching a crescendo as we confess that Jesus is . . .

> ". . . the Only Begotten Son of God, born of the Father before all ages. God from God, Light from Light, true God from true God, begotten, not made, CONSUBSTANTIAL WITH THE FATHER; THROUGH HIM ALL THINGS WERE MADE."

There is a reason the church fathers spent centuries debating and agonizing to get these words right: they knew that the key to proclaiming the gospel is to ensure that Jesus is authentic (God from God) and can be trusted (true God from true God). If we are about to make a huge investment of money, we want to know beyond the shadow of a doubt that we are investing in a credible, authentic source. At the heart of our catechetical ministry is the invitation to invest one's whole heart, soul, mind, and strength in the Person of Jesus Christ. It is our job to present Jesus as trustworthy, and we ourselves must embody those qualities that establish trust so that when we invite people to consider this better way, they feel that their investment is safe.

> **At the heart of our catechetical ministry is the invitation to invest one's whole heart, soul, mind, and strength in the Person of Jesus Christ.**

True Tales

When I served as a catechist at Most Holy Redeemer parish in Evergreen Park (just outside of Chicago), the Director of Religious Education, Arlene Astrowski, required that we present a group covenant on the first day of sessions and invite all participants to come forward and sign it in a prayerful ritual. This was designed to establish a climate of trust that would enable all participants to feel safe and secure in sharing their faith with one another. After everyone signed the group covenant, it was to be displayed each week during sessions and referred to whenever behaviors occurred that violated what all had agreed to. Here is the text of that group covenant (for elementary-age children) which you are free to use and adapt:

I have the right to be HAPPY and to be treated with KINDNESS in this group. I have the responsibility to treat others with kindness.

This means that no one will LAUGH at me, IGNORE me, or HURT my feelings, and I am responsible to behave accordingly with others.

I have the right to be MYSELF in this group. This means that no one will treat me UNFAIRLY because I am FAT OR THIN, FAST OR SLOW, BOY OR GIRL. I have the responsibility to show this same respect to others.

I have the right to HEAR and be HEARD in this group. This means that no one will YELL, SCREAM, OR SHOUT. My opinion and needs will be considered in any plans we make. I have the responsibility to respectfully listen to others.

I have a right in this group to learn about MYSELF. This means that I will be free to express my feelings and opinions without being interrupted or punished. I have the responsibility to respect the feelings and opinions of others and to not interrupt them.

I have a right to be ME, to learn about ME, about OTHERS, and about GOD. I have the responsibility to see to it that others can do the same.

I commit to RESPECTING your RIGHTS and MINE and RESPECTING the property in this learning space. I will not destroy, write on, or misuse the property in this space, because I do not want anyone to destroy the things that belong to me.

Questions for Reflection and Discussion

> What does it mean to say that, in terms of following the better way offered by Jesus, we are incapable of "getting there" on our own and need "divine intervention"?

> How can the Incarnation—the fact that God sent his only Son to become one of us—be thought of as an intervention? What dysfunction did Jesus come to deal with? What does it mean to say that following Jesus' better way is akin to "living in recovery"?

> When, where, how, and through whom did you first encounter Jesus Christ?
> How comfortable are you talking to others about your relationship with Jesus Christ?
> How has the clergy sex abuse scandal and its cover-up affected your own level of trust in the Church? How has it affected others you know?
> How emotionally safe do you feel in your work (or school or other) environment? Choose a leader from this environment and complete the Trust Equation described on page 17 for him or her. Which of the four factors is strongest? Which is most lacking?
> Invite a trusted individual to complete the Trust Equation on your behalf and reflect and discuss the results and how you can grow in your ability to establish trust.
> Of the twelve skills listed and described for establishing a climate of trust (pages 18-19), which are your strongest? In which might you improve?

Scripture

Here is a trustworthy saying: Whoever aspires to be an overseer desires a noble task. Now the overseer is to be above reproach, faithful to his wife, temperate, self-controlled, respectable, hospitable, able to teach, not given to drunkenness, not violent but gentle, not quarrelsome, not a lover of money. He must manage his own family well and see that his children obey him, and he must do so in a manner worthy of full respect. 1 TIMOTHY 3:1–4

Prayer

Lord, you have called me to the noble task of overseeing those who seek to know you better. Help me to be trustworthy and to create a learning environment in which participants feel safe, respected, and comfortable so that they might open their minds and hearts to your grace. Amen.

Chapter 3

Tell of Jesus' Mighty Deeds—
Past and Present

Some years ago, a TV commercial for a food-processing appliance proudly proclaimed that this innovation "slices, dices, and makes julienne fries!" Today, people continue to recall that phrase and use it, tongue-in-cheek, when describing the amazing capabilities of any new gadget. This phrase and others like it is emblematic of what is known as the "advertis-

> When Jesus came on the scene 2,000 years ago, he started his mission by making a startling claim.

ing claim"—the part of the ad that seeks to create a perception of superiority. It is the job of the advertiser to convince consumers by providing evidence of this superiority. And so, products offer evidence that they are stronger, faster-acting, easier, more effective, longer-lasting, and better-tasting.

When Jesus came on the scene 2,000 years ago, he started his mission by making a startling claim. He stood up in the synagogue in Nazareth and read the following passage from Isaiah:

Living Up to the Hype

Political campaign ads make a lot of claims: they emphasize the candidate's capabilities (often based on past accomplishments) in order to appeal to voters. On a more personal level, when you and I prepare our résumé and/or interview for a job, we play up our talents, skills, and capabilities, accompanied by stories of past accomplishments in order to convince the employer that we are worth the risk of hiring. In all these cases, it behooves us to be able to live up to the claims we make!

"The Spirit of the Lord is on me, / because he has anointed me / to proclaim good news to the poor. / He has sent me to proclaim freedom for the prisoners / and recovery of sight for the blind, / to set the oppressed free, / to proclaim the year of the Lord's favor" (Luke 4:18–19).

He then proclaimed: "Today this scripture is fulfilled in your hearing" (Luke 4:21). That's the startling part. Jesus claimed that he was the fulfillment of the greatest hopes and desires of God's people. When the imprisoned John the Baptist sought confirmation that Jesus was the "real thing," Jesus replied, "Go back and report to John what you have seen and heard: The blind receive sight, the lame walk, those who have leprosy are cleansed, the deaf hear, the dead are raised, and the good news is proclaimed to the poor" (Luke 7:22).

Proclaiming Jesus' Amazing Deeds

Proclaiming the Good News of Jesus necessitates proclaiming his amazing deeds. On Pentecost, in the first proclamation of the gospel—known as the *kerygma*—Peter wasted no time in recalling Jesus' amazing deeds: "Fellow Israelites, listen to this: Jesus of Nazareth was a man accredited by God to you by miracles, wonders and signs, which God did among you through him, as you yourselves know" (Acts 2:22).

> Proclaiming the Good News of Jesus necessitates proclaiming his amazing deeds.

When we proclaim the Good News of Jesus, we must remember that those to whom we proclaim are wondering, "Who is this Jesus? What has he done?" and "What can he do for me?" In order for us to prepare people's hearts and minds, it is incumbent on us to tell the stories of Jesus' amazing deeds, beginning with the stories we have in Scripture in which he opens the eyes of the blind, heals the sick, changes water into wine, calms the storm, and raises people from the dead. But

we must not stop there; if we truly want to loosen the soil of people's hearts and minds, we must tell the stories of the amazing things that Jesus has done and is doing for us *in our very own lives*! We need to share how Jesus has transformed us, healed us (whether physically, emotionally, or spiritually), raised us to new life, and enabled us to live a better way.

Think of what happens when you go to purchase a brand-new car or some other major investment. If you're like me, you go in with an attitude of reluctance, avoiding any indication that you are eager to make a purchase. The pressure is on the salesperson to show his or her knowledge of the product and to wow you with the details of what the product can do. His or her job is to convince you that you need this product and that can't be done without full knowledge of the product's capabilities. The same holds true for us as disciples of Jesus Christ. We are dealing with people, many of whom are reluctant to invest in Jesus. It is our job to convince them that having Jesus in their lives will be a game-changer. For us to do this, we must be able to talk about the Person of Jesus Christ and describe what he has done and is doing for those who seek his help. In doing so, we are prompting—even enticing—people to "place" Jesus in their "cart"—the step before proceeding to "checkout!"

> We must be able to talk about the Person of Jesus Christ and describe what Jesus has done and is doing for those who seek his help.

The key, however, is to remember that we are about the business of proclaiming God, not just a set of concepts, beliefs, or principles. We are not teachers of a subject but are facilitators of an encounter. Think about it: there is a big difference between telling someone about a celebrity you have researched and introducing them to a celebrity you know personally! And, how do we get to know Jesus personally? Through prayerful encounters with the stories of the gospels. As catechists, we must introduce those we teach to the Jesus of the gospels, making these stories the centerpiece of our catechesis. Too often, our catechesis takes the form of well-intentioned and highly organized lectures, but lectures nonetheless—outlines and bullet points of principles and concepts that summarize Jesus' message. Jesus, on the other hand, taught most often by telling stories and by performing actions that became stories in and of themselves. If we want to proclaim the great deeds of the Lord in a way that touches the hearts of those we teach, we need to reclaim the art of storytelling and invite those we teach to reflect on the stories of the Gospels as a way of encountering Jesus.

Stories Lead to Insight, Action, and Ultimately Faith

One of the foremost experts on the art of storytelling in recent times, prolific author and speaker Jack Shea, reminds us that our storytelling of Jesus begins with this mindset:

> "What has He done for me? He has loved me and given me His whole self. What shall I do for Him? I shall love Him and give myself to Him without reserve."
> —St. Ignatius of Loyola

> I never saw him. I never heard him. I never touched him. But there were those who did. And they told others, who told others, who told others still, who eventually told me. And now, in my turn, I tell you. And you, then, can tell others. And so, you see, there will never be an end to it. (*An Experience Named Spirit*)

Shea asserts that the "memory of Jesus is necessary to discern the present activity of the Spirit." If we hope to lead those we teach to encounter Jesus Christ in the present, we must powerfully proclaim the Gospel stories that convey his memory. The stories of Jesus' amazing deeds constitute our tradition. However, that tradition must be transmitted by living and breathing human beings—by catechists. Our goal is to establish and facilitate a dialogue with Scripture that enables the stories of the past to speak to the experiences of the present. Shea goes on to emphasize why stories are so effective: they are interesting, they are accessible, they convey meaning, they stress the initiative of God, they introduce "God-language," they create images, they generate further storytelling, and they lead to insights and action and ultimately, to faith.

Storytelling creates what Christian author Nate Wilson refers to as "the aroma of the gospel." An aroma, of course, is something that surrounds us, penetrates us, and lingers with us. To effectively create the "aroma of the gospel" through storytelling, we need to pay attention to several key elements.

Storytelling creates "the aroma of the gospel."

Biblical Animation: Not About Cartoons

There is a movement afoot in the worldwide church to ensure that all ministry is "biblically animated." This is not to be confused with drawings or cartoons of Bible stories. To be "biblically animated" is to say that our ministry is powered, or animated, by Scripture. The foundation of our ministry—in this case, catechesis/faith formation—is the story of our salvation through Jesus Christ, a story revealed to us in Scripture. Biblically animated ministry always includes a proclamation of Scripture. If we hope to introduce others to Jesus Christ, we must proclaim the stories of Scripture that reveal how God rescues, restores, and reassures his people through his Son. Therefore, growing in knowledge of Scripture should be at the top of every catechist's wish list. Catechists must be biblically animated.

+ **Preparation.** To be a good storyteller, you need to do your homework. By all means, read the story (several times, in fact) ahead of time and enter it yourself, allowing it to speak to you and for you to get to know the story. Then, be sure to focus on the main point of the story that you wish to draw attention to. You may even consider recording yourself telling the story so that you can review it and make adjustments. Finally, the most powerful way to tell a story is to memorize it and tell it from memory instead of just reading it.

+ **Create a world.** Like a video game that creates a world for players to enter, an effective storyteller creates a world for listeners to enter with their imaginations. Consider using props, sound effects, art, and music. Use your voice, facial expression, and body language to indicate different speakers in the story. Maximize your storytelling space by moving around, and include audience participation when possible.

> **Tell me the facts and I'll learn. Tell me the truth and I'll believe. But tell me a story and it will live in my heart forever.**
> —NATIVE AMERICAN PROVERB

➕ **Use nonverbal communication.** Some of the most effective storytelling is done through nonverbal expressions. Don't just use your voice to tell a story; use your whole body! Think about your posture, how you use your eyes (making expressions and making eye contact with various participants), and how you move about the space.

➕ **Use your voice as a tool.** Storytelling is not just a matter of reading a story; you need to tell a story with your voice. That means paying attention to volume (rising and falling to create drama) as well as to pace, silence, pauses, and tone.

> **An effective storyteller creates a world for listeners to enter with their imaginations.**

Here is a script of a dramatized telling of a Gospel story (Jesus heals Jairus's daughter) from Loyola Press's *Finding God* Grade 5 catechist manual (based on Mark 5:21–24, 35–43). As you read through it, think of all the ways you would use the above strategies (movement, gestures, facial expression, voice, pauses) to engage your participants with this story.

Jesus was teaching by the Sea of Galilee, when an official from the synagogue broke through the large crowd. The official's name was Jairus. When he saw Jesus, he knelt down in front of him. But he was so upset he could hardly speak. "My daughter is dying!" cried Jairus. "Please come see her. I know that if you place your hands upon her and pray to God, she will get well."

Jesus agreed to go with Jairus, but while they were still on their way, some people who had just been to Jairus's house met them on the road. "It's too late, Jairus," they said. "Your daughter has just died. There's no need for the Teacher to come now. Why bother him with this?"

Jairus looked as if he could collapse in his grief, but Jesus took his arm quickly. "Never mind what they say," Jesus told him. "Now is not the time for fear—have faith, Jairus." Jesus raised his voice then, to be heard by the crowd of people who were following them. "The rest of you go home. Peter, James, John—I want only you three to come into the house with me."

(continued on next page)

So, the rest of the crowd stood back and let the small group of men go on their way. When they got to the house, people were wailing and crying, causing a big scene. "Why all this commotion?" Jesus asked. "The child hasn't died—she's just asleep."

"Who could say such a cruel thing!" exclaimed a bystander. "Are you crazy? The girl is dead—I watched her take her last breaths!" Another bystander yelled, "Get this man out of here—he just walked in and he's talking like he knows more than we do. This family has been through enough!"

Jesus calmly responded, "All of you leave. Give us some time alone. Go on . . ." So, everyone left except Jesus, Peter, James, John, Jairus, and his wife. They went to the room where the child was lying. Jesus sat next to her and leaned close to her pale face and closed eyes. Gently, he took her hand. "Little girl, get up!" Jesus commanded. As soon as Jesus spoke the words, the child got out of bed and began to walk around. She was only 12 years old.

Jairus exclaimed, "Oh! Oh! She's alive!" His wife shouted, "Praise God!" The girl came to Jesus and hugged him. He smiled down at her and stroked her hair. But his eyes were stern when he looked at her parents. "It's very important that you not tell anyone what happened here." Jesus said. "They would misunderstand."

Jairus replied, "Yes, good Teacher. We'll do whatever you say." Jesus smiled then and gently led the child back to her parents' arms. "Your daughter will be fine now, but the illness has made her weak." Jesus aid. "Give her something to eat."

Nix the "Once Upon a Time . . ."

One more piece of advice: Do not begin a Scripture story with "Once upon a time . . ." That phrase will serve to trivialize what you are about to say and reduce it to a fairy tale. Just tell your audience that you are going to tell them a story, pause, and then launch into it. Likewise, do not say, "the end" at the conclusion of the story. Just speak the last line of the story and let it "sit there."

Speaking the Language of the Kingdom

Storytelling is one of the ways we "speak" in the kingdom of God. Matthew Halbach writes that these powerful stories "take us out of our comfort zone and transport us to the fringes of reality—the threshold between our world and the kingdom of God—where the difference between our thoughts and our ways and those of God is mournfully clear" ("What Parables Can Teach the Synod Fathers and the Church Today," *Catechetical Leader*, March 2015). Stories do this by achieving the following. They invite the listener to . . .

Storytelling is one of the ways we "speak" in the kingdom of God.

- ✚ consider an alternative reality.
- ✚ enter a relationship with the storyteller.
- ✚ encounter the mind of God.
- ✚ consider a counterintuitive way of thinking.
- ✚ embrace a future that is underway and can't be stopped.
- ✚ follow Jesus more closely.
- ✚ contemplate repentance.
- ✚ deepen commitment.

It's important that we don't stop there, however. It is not enough to tell the stories of what Jesus did in the past. We must continue to weave a narrative that our participants can enter—a narrative that continuously describes Jesus acting in the lives of his people down through the ages (which is why we tell stories of the lives of the saints!) and into the present day, including

A catechist was doing her best to dramatically tell the Old Testament story of Lot's wife, who turned into a pillar of salt when she looked back. Suddenly, a boy in her group raised his hand and shouted excitedly, "Something like that happened to my mom last week!" When the catechist asked him to explain, he said, "She looked back once while she was driving." The catechist asked, "What happened to her?" The boy replied, "She turned into a telephone pole."

The Myths of Storytelling

What's holding us back from more effectively using the power of stories to make disciples? According to Christian author, evangelizer, and storyteller Christine Dillon, we have to break through a number of myths about storytelling, such as adults won't listen to stories, stories are only for non-literate cultures, men won't listen to stories, stories won't grow mature disciples, storytelling will lead to heresy, storytelling is too slow a method, and more (*Stories Aren't Just for Kids*). She also asserts, quite correctly, that many of those to whom we proclaim the gospel are biblically illiterate and that we cannot assume they know the stories of the gospels. (*Telling the Gospel Through Story: Evangelism That Keeps Hearers Wanting More*) If, as the New Evangelization suggests, we are going to "re-propose" the gospel to our culture, that will necessitate re-proposing Scripture stories themselves.

in our own lives. This means that we need to tell stories of what Jesus has done for us when we have experienced powerlessness, pain, emptiness, anxiety, despair, and so on, as well as how we have encountered him in moments of great joy—any experience that led to a significant transition in our lives. If you want to share your own story of how you have encountered Jesus, look to tell stories about how you have encountered the Lord through experiences such as these:

- a change in job status
- an engagement or marriage
- becoming a parent
- a change in residence
- dealing with an addiction (yours or a loved one's)
- surviving any form of abuse
- going away to college
- losing a loved one
- taking on a difficult project
- a challenging volunteer experience
- a vacation

- a lack of rest, sleep, or recreation
- an increase in responsibilities
- becoming an empty nester
- a change in health (such as injury or illness)
- a change in your financial situation
- retirement (your own or your spouse's)
- a loved one being sent to war
- a grown child leaving home
- caring for an aging parent
- a major change in diet
- facing a conflict
- encountering legal troubles
- a major achievement
- the blending of families
- reaching a milestone
- visiting a place of great natural beauty
- a divorce or the end of a relationship
- an experience of failure
- a near-death experience
- dealing with chronic pain
- moments of intense joy
- a loved one announces they are gay
- receiving a reprimand

If you and I are going to be more evangelizing catechists who hope to prepare people's hearts and minds, we need to pause and ask ourselves, "What great things has Jesus done for me?" and then we need to tell those stories. Spend some time in prayer, asking Jesus to help you see the ways he has touched your life, transformed you, and healed you. And then, ask him to help you tell your story and to invite others to get in touch with their own stories.

> We must ask ourselves, "What great things has Jesus done for me?"

Talking Like TED

As a church, we need to take our cue from the highly successful TED talks, which effectively persuade and inspire countless numbers of people to transformation of mind and heart on a variety of topics. How do they do it? Not by lecturing or debating but through effective storytelling. The experts behind TED talks say that a good TED talk is about two-thirds storytelling, while the other one-third is informative data usually provided in no more than three "chunks."

Storytelling: Jesus' Preferred Method

We don't make disciples of Jesus Christ by engaging others in debate or by lecturing them about principles of dogma or through apologetics, as important as those tools may be later in the process of catechesis. Jesus' preferred method of engaging others and teaching about the reign of God was through storytelling. People are more open to hearing a story about an everyday experience in which God's nearness is revealed. If we are going to prepare them for the Good News, we've got to learn to become storytellers, because stories have been and continue to be one of the most effective ways of sparking the imagination, which is what happens when one encounters Christ.

Unfortunately, imagination sometimes is misunderstood—and mistrusted. We think of the imagination as being out of touch with reality when—in reality—imagination is our capacity to see beyond to the greater reality. Really. In a sense, imagination is the key to navigating, deciphering, and transcending the reality that meets the eye so that we can recognize unseen reality ("all that is visible and invisible"). Imagination is at the heart of the gospel message because stories are at the heart of the gospel. Ultimately, Jesus' wildly imaginative proclamation of the reign of God is much more than the proposal of a preferred way of seeing reality: it is an invitation to an indispensable way of seeing. In essence, imagination is a prerequisite for hope. To be imaginative is to develop a way of approaching reality that, while not contrary to reason, goes beyond reason and brings us into contact with mystery. Author

> Imagination is at the heart of the gospel message because stories are at the heart of the gospels.

John Shea describes the prominent role of imagination in spirituality when he says, "Thinking is the furniture and imagination is the room. We can rearrange the furniture all we want but sometimes what we need is a larger room" (*Stories of Faith*). Storytelling is the art of building a bigger room!

The stories we tell are not frivolous, nor are they for purposes of entertaining. They embody the great deeds of the Lord. Actions are in direct correlation to a person's heart and mind. Throughout Scripture, God reveals his heart and mind, not only by what he says but primarily by his loving actions, not the least of which include creation, the establishment of his covenant, the liberation of the Jews from slavery, and the countless times he forgives his people despite their unfaithfulness. Jesus, likewise, is known by his actions, not the least of which include his miracles, his time spent with outcasts, his forgiveness of sins and, ultimately, his passion, death, and Resurrection. These are the stories we tell. If we want the people we teach

> To be imaginative is to develop a way of approaching reality that, while not contrary to reason, goes beyond reason and brings us into contact with mystery.

to encounter Christ, we need to tell them about Jesus' amazing deeds and, if we want to do that effectively, we need to communicate that information in story form.

True Tales

When I was teaching a unit on morality to eighth graders, we were exploring the seventh and eighth Commandments about not stealing or bearing false witness against our neighbor. I told the kids a story about when I was in eighth grade, working with a group of four other classmates on a science project involving saltwater fish. Our teacher Sister Laurenta gave us permission to walk over to the pet shop during lunch (something you could do back in the day!) to purchase some of our supplies. While we were there, the owner told us he had to go in the back to find one of the items we requested. When he disappeared into the back room, the leader of our group said to the rest of us, "Hey, watch this!" and he proceeded to grab several bags of aquarium salt and stuff them into his jacket. The rest of us watched, dumbfounded; we had never seen anyone shoplift, let alone someone we knew. The owner came out, and we nervously completed our transaction and left the store without the owner noticing what was missing. Or so we thought. Later that day, the owner called the school and said that he suspected a group of boys from the school had shoplifted. Sister Laurenta called us in one by one to ask us what had happened and if we saw someone take the bags of salt. And how did young Joey Paprocki reply when Sister asked him? "Oh no, Sister! I didn't see anything like that!" Now, it was the turn for the young people to whom I was speaking to be dumbfounded. "You did that?" gasped one of the students. "Yes, I did. And I'm not at all proud of it. I helped a friend steal, and I lied to a person in authority." From that point on, I noticed that the kids saw me differently. Until then, they seemed to tolerate me at best and dismiss what I had to say at worst. Admitting my faults to them by way of a story gave me credibility in their eyes. I was not perfect. I was someone who struggled like they did to do the right thing. That experience taught me that storytelling can penetrate in a way that a lecture never could. It is especially helpful to share stories of our own failures and brokenness, because the young people we teach tend to think that we are boring adults who have never broken the rules or done anything wrong.

Questions for Reflection and Discussion

> Think of a TV commercial that makes amazing claims about what a product or service can do. Think of a candidate for political office who has made amazing claims of what he or she will do if elected. What is the purpose of making such amazing claims?
> What startling claim did Jesus make when he got up to speak in the synagogue in Nazareth? Why was this claim so startling?
> When John's disciples asked for proof that Jesus was the messiah, how did Jesus reply?
> What are your favorite Gospel stories of Jesus' mighty deeds?
> What does it mean to say that we catechists are not teachers of a subject but rather, facilitators of an encounter with a person? What difference does it make?
> Who was/is a great storyteller in your life? Why are stories such an effective medium for communicating?
> How can you use stories to more effectively tell of Jesus' mighty deeds? What skills do you possess when it comes to storytelling? What skills do you need to strengthen?
> What great thing(s) has Jesus done for you personally?

Scripture

The disciples came to [Jesus] and asked, "Why do you speak to the people in parables?" He replied, "Because the knowledge of the secrets of the kingdom of heaven has been given to you, but not to them." MATTHEW 13:10–11

Prayer

Lord Jesus, help me reflect on all the wonderful things you have done for me and for others so that I may tell the stories of your great deeds. Help me become a good storyteller so that hearts may be touched and lives may be changed. Amen.

Chapter 4

Introduce the Key to New Life: Laying Down One's Life

It is a fairly common practice in advertising to garner attention by making a claim about a product or service that is counterintuitive or defies commonly accepted reasoning. For example:

- a diet plan promises you can lose weight in 30 days while eating all the bacon you want;
- a light beer promises robust flavor with only 64 calories;
- a body lotion promises to physically reshape your body;
- a bracelet promises to relieve arthritic pain.

The Key to Eternal Life Is . . .

While these claims sound too good to be true, they also pique our curiosity. We want to see for ourselves, kind of like when the apostle Thomas heard the other apostles claim that Jesus was risen from the dead. Thomas replied that he needed to see this for himself, and boy, was he treated to a personal demonstration (John 20:24–29).

At the heart of our proclamation of the better way of Jesus is a claim that defies all reasonable thinking: **The key to eternal life is dying!** We basically ask of those we teach, "Can I interest you in eternal life?" and when people express interest, we show them a crucified man. We proclaim the paschal mystery, which teaches that death is not the end but is the key to transformation that brings new

> At the heart of our proclamation of the better way of Jesus is a claim that defies all reasonable thinking: The key to eternal life is dying!

life. And it begins with laying down one's own life. For us to effectively prepare people's hearts and minds, we need to teach people of all ages how to *lay down their lives*. Jesus said, "Greater love has no one than this: to lay down one's life for one's friends" (John 15:13). Jesus, of course, laid down his life for us. Over the centuries of church history, many martyrs have laid down their lives for their faith. And, of course, many military personnel as well as first responders have laid down their lives for others. Teachers have laid down their lives to save their students from mass shootings.

What about the rest of us? Is the "greatest love" out of reach for the average person because we have not and probably will not physically die or be killed because of our faith? Unfortunately, we have too narrowly defined what it means to lay down your life for others. While some, like Jesus, die a physical death for others, the rest of us are called to lay down our lives for others each and every day. To die for others is the ultimate example, but **to lay down your life means to set your own needs aside to tend to the needs of others. This is the heart of the message we proclaim. It is the heart of what we know as the paschal mystery.**

> To lay down your life means to set your own needs aside to tend to the needs of others.

We are called to lay down our lives every day. Parents and spouses set aside their own needs to tend to the needs of their children, one another, and perhaps their aging parents. Teachers and catechists set aside their own needs to tend to the needs of their students. Doctors and nurses set aside their own needs to tend to the needs of their patients. Workers set aside their own needs to tend to the needs of their customers or coworkers. And so on. It is our job as catechists to teach people how to lay down their lives. In Ignatian spirituality, this is simply known as being "people for others." We instill this notion of being people for others by providing our learners with opportunities to practice selfless love. Whether we call them service projects, mercy experiences, people-for-others projects, or something else, we must be about the work of apprenticing those we teach in acts of selfless love—the laying down their lives for others.

An Apprenticeship in Selfless Love

Several years ago, I served as a sixth-grade catechist at a parish in which the catechetical leader asked every grade level to involve kids in a service experience. I arranged for the young people to prepare and serve dinner for parents and families of hospitalized children at a local Ronald McDonald House. They thoroughly enjoyed the experience. At the end of the year, when I asked them what they liked best about religious education that year, every one of them identified the service experience as their favorite moment. (I thought that I taught some pretty awesome classes that year, but they obviously paled in comparison!) It is no surprise that this was their favorite moment, because their hearts were touched, and they were able to put into action what they were being taught. They had an experience of laying down their lives and, in doing so, discovered new life. The experience tilled the soil of their hearts and minds. One sixth-grade boy even told me that he asked his parents if they could volunteer there as a family sometime soon. As evangelizing catechists, we need to do more than indoctrinate; we need to instigate! We need to mobilize people to participate in works that are characterized by setting their own needs aside and tend to the needs of others.

> As evangelizing catechists, we need to do more than indoctrinate; we need to instigate!

Faith formation should resemble nothing less than an apprenticeship in selfless love, because selfless love is the very essence of God; it is a love that always seeks the good of the other. To engage in selfless love is to enter the life of the Trinity—a community of love so selfless that God is one—and our faith formation should seek to do nothing less than to lead those we teach into the life of God.

At the end of the previous chapter, we pointed out that people are known by their actions. Ultimately, this is how God has revealed himself to us over the ages: through God's actions. And if those actions can be summarized in one word, that word would be *selfless*. While Scripture tells us that God is love, it is important for us to remember that love is not just one characteristic of God but rather is God's *very essence*. Likewise, it is important to know that the love that God exemplifies is a certain kind of love: it is selfless love. The Greek word for love that is used in the New Testament

> We are formed and molded by our thoughts. Those whose minds are shaped by selfless thoughts give joy when they speak or act. Joy follows them like a shadow that never leaves them.
> —THE BUDDHA

is *agape,* which goes beyond sensual/romantic (*eros*), beyond affectionate/familial (*storge*), and beyond intimate/emotional (*philia*). Agape love is perfectly unconditional and selfless. It is God's very nature to be self-giving. This notion is summed up in that famous Gospel verse John 3:16: "For God so loved the world that he gave his one and only Son, that whoever believes in him shall not perish but have eternal life." God's love for the world is manifested by giving of himself. God's love is not some kind of a vague feeling of affection nor is it just some kind of abstract notion.

For people made in the image and likeness of God, selfless love is shown through charity and justice: through radical concern for the ultimate well-being of all God's people. Throughout history, many people have exemplified this self-giving love of God for his people. One contemporary example was Dorothy Day. If Dorothy Day stood for anything, it was the centrality of the works of mercy in the life of Catholics. She once said that everything a baptized person does should be directly or indirectly related to the corporal and spiritual works of mercy. Unlike some who reduce Christianity to a philosophy,

God's Actions Speak Loudly

God's love is characterized by concrete actions of giving, even when the recipient is undeserving or has done nothing to earn such love:

> God gave us all of creation.
> God gave Adam and Eve clothes to wear upon their leaving the Garden.
> God gave Cain a mark to protect him after he murdered his brother, Abel.
> God gave freedom to the enslaved Jewish people.
> God gave manna in the desert to his people.
> God gave his Law to his people.
> God gave the Promised Land to his people.
> God gave his people kings to lead them.
> God gave his people prophets to guide them.
> God gave the world his only Son, Jesus Christ.
> God gave the Holy Spirit to the church.

It is no wonder, then, that God insists that his children—made in his image and likeness—love one another in the same selfless, self-giving fashion in which God has loved us.

Dorothy Day knew that Christianity was an embodied set of practices: things that we *do* for others. When we engage in works of mercy, we set aside our ego and shift our focus to the needs of others. This is not just a nice thing we do as Christians; it is what defines us (or at least should).

> God insists that his children—made in his image and likeness—love one another in the same selfless, self-giving fashion in which God has loved us.

This is precisely why we incorporate service components in our catechetical programs. In the spirit of Dorothy Day, however, I propose that we stop referring to these components as "service hours" or "service projects" but rather call them "**mercy experiences.**" Public schools require service hours as a way of developing good citizens and instilling an upright ethical attitude. Catholics engage in service as a way of extending God's loving mercy to others, sharing one another's burdens, and "moving in sync with the deepest rhythms of creation" (*The Strangest Way*, Bishop Robert Barron, 153). As such, these works are not service projects nor service hours but rather are experiences of God's enduring mercy and selfless love.

> Above all the grace and the gifts that Christ gives to his beloved is that of overcoming self.
> St. Francis of Assisi

Sacrificial Love

The love that Jesus exemplified by dying on the cross is not only selfless; it is *sacrificial*. Archbishop Fulton Sheen described God's love as sacrificial: "So the divine love is sacrificial love. Love does not mean to have and to own and to possess. It means to be had and to be owned and to be possessed. It is not a circle circumscribed by self, it is arms outstretched to embrace all humanity within its grasp." The word *sacrifice* comes from the Latin which means "to make holy," and to be holy means to be like God because God alone is holy. To love someone involves making sacrifices for them; it means to set aside our own needs to put the needs of the other first. It is love without keeping score. It is love that is proactive.

If we're waiting until eighth grade or high school confirmation classes to involve young people in service hours/mercy experiences, we're waiting too long and allowing the soil to become compacted! From the very beginning of faith formation—including adults in RCIA—participants should be invited to participate in mercy experiences, experiences of selfless love in which they lay down their lives for the lives of others. This is the most effective way to loosen the soil of people's hearts. Dying and rising is the central truth of our faith. There is no getting around the cross; it is the key to fullness of life.

> If we're waiting until eighth grade or high school confirmation classes to involve young people in service/mercy experiences, we're waiting too long.

Service as Part of the "Core Curriculum"

A good example of a faith-formation program that is embracing this notion of self-giving love as the heart of its curriculum is at St. Joseph Parish in Manchester, MO. The parish website "advertises" service opportunities as one of the hallmarks of its program beginning in early childhood classes. Some of their service experiences include:

✚ **Early Childhood Learning Center:** Collects gently used and new books and stuffed animals for Ready to Learn.

✚ **Kindergarten:** Make and send get-well cards to parishioners who are sick.

✚ **First grade:** Make craft kits for Shriners Hospital so that the patients may create their own crafts, and collect new coloring books, markers, crayons, and small games for them as well.

✚ **Second grade:** Make fleece blankets to be donated to Nurses for Newborns.

✚ **Third grade:** Engage in a pen pal correspondence between the children and older parishioners.

✚ **Fourth grade:** Make sandwiches in November for the Winter Shelter Sandwich Program and organize a book drive after the first of the year for St. Augustine's School in Wellston.

✚ **Fifth grade:** Organize a used shoe collection for Clean Water Mission to raise funds needed to drill wells for water in various disadvantaged countries.

+ **Sixth grade:** Engage in various behind-the-scenes service activities that involve sacramental programs in our parish; help with diaper drive for Mary Queen of the Angels; help with the junior high leaf-raking project.

+ **Seventh grade:** Partner with West County Care Center; students rotate to visit and help orchestrate a bowling activity or games with the residents; also rake leaves on the parish grounds in the fall.

+ **Eighth grade:** Beginning in September and ending in May, 5–6 students will partner with the St. Joseph's Knights of Columbus to work at the Mother Teresa Soup Kitchen on the second and fifth Mondays of each month. They will also rake leaves for elderly parishioners and parishioners in need in the fall.

Ten members of a Jesuit high school debate team survived a terrible plane crash but were left dangling off a cliff, clinging to a long thin branch. The silver-tongued team captain was able to hold on with one arm and, using his free hand, grabbed his cell phone and called the school's chaplain—a Jesuit priest and former physics teacher. The captain described their precarious situation, explaining that there were 10 students clinging to a branch that was 15 feet long but only 3 inches thick. The priest responded, "There's no way that branch will sustain the weight of all ten of you. Someone will have to make the supreme sacrifice to save the others. You've been taught to be people for others. Use your great persuasive speaking skills to inspire them. In the meantime, I'll call for rescuers." The captain said he understood, put the phone away, and gave a passionate, inspirational speech about being people for others and how one of them must make the ultimate sacrifice so that the others could be saved. A few minutes later, the priest's phone rang. Seeing that it was the team captain, he quickly answered the call and asked for an update. The team captain said, "I made the most impassioned and inspirational speech of my life just as you told me, but unfortunately, I'm the only one left!" The priest anxiously asked, "Well, what happened?!" to which the captain responded, "When I finished my speech, they applauded."

A Director of Corporal Works of Mercy?

The website of a Catholic parish in Poway, California, reveals that the parish pastoral staff includes a *Director of the Corporal Works of Mercy*! Would that all parishes had such a position on staff!

In my book, *A Church on the Move: 52 Ways to Get Mission and Mercy in Motion*, I went as far as to propose that religious education curricula shift from the traditional focus on doctrinal themes for each year of faith formation and instead focus on themes drawn from the works of mercy and Catholic social teaching.

Traditional Doctrinal Curriculum	Curriculum Based on Works of Mercy and CST
Grade 1: God	Grade 1: Care for God's Creation
Grade 2: First Reconciliation and First Eucharist	Grade 2: Feeding the Hungry/Giving Drink to the Thirsty
Grade 3: Church	Grade 3: Call to Family, Community, Participation
Grade 4: Ten Commandments/ Morality	Grade 4: Clothing the Naked
Grade 5: The Seven Sacraments	Grade 5: Sheltering the Homeless
Grade 6: Old Testament	Grade 6: Option for the Poor and Vulnerable
Grade 7: Jesus/New Testament	Grade 7: Visiting the Sick
Grade 8: Church History and/or Confirmation	Grade 8: Solidarity

Finally, if we are truly going to prepare people's hearts by involving them in works of mercy, we need to do so by focusing on mentoring and apprenticeship. This idea is nothing new: the role of the sponsor at baptism is a long and valued tradition in the Catholic Church. In the Rite of Christian Initiation for Adults, those who are seeking to enter full communion with the Catholic Church are to be provided a sponsor whose responsibility is "to show the candidates how to practice the Gospel in personal and social life" (RCIA 75). The sponsor is not the one

If we are truly going to prepare people's hearts by involving them in works of mercy, we need to do so by focusing on mentoring and apprenticeship.

who teaches the candidate all the dogmas and doctrines of the Catholic Church. This role belongs to the catechist. Rather, the sponsor is someone who helps the candidate become more familiar with the Christian way of life, helping by example and support so that the candidate might turn "more readily to prayer, to bear witness to the faith, in all things to keep their hopes set on Christ, to follow supernatural inspiration in their deeds, and to practice love of neighbor" (RCIA 75–2).

In recent centuries, the Catholic Church has not fully tapped the rich potential of the role of the sponsor and thus of the mentor-apprentice relationship. A spiritual mentor is a committed Catholic who shares with another, less-experienced Catholic (or someone interested in becoming Catholic) how he or she practices the faith in daily living. A mentor is not a problem solver but a companion on a journey. Communication is the key to this relationship. The mentor has no professional training. Rather, the relationship is based on experience, gratitude, trust, and a shared desire to follow Jesus more closely.

The Essentials of an Apprenticeship

Years ago, it was common for a young person to learn a trade by being apprenticed to someone who was a master in that trade. When it was published in 1997, the *General Directory for Catechesis* created some excitement by declaring that faith formation was to be understood as an apprenticeship (paragraph 67). Just what does it mean to apprentice someone into the Catholic faith? To answer that, let's look at the essentials of an apprenticeship.

- ✚ The goal of an apprenticeship is for the apprentice to work closely with a skilled mentor to learn essential knowledge and skills needed for the trade.

- ✚ Apprenticeships involve hands-on work accompanied by study (classroom learning).

- ✚ Apprentices are considered full-time employees who are learning on-the-job.

- ✚ Apprenticeships often last several years but are often competency-based (with specific goals identified) rather than just time-based.

- ✚ The apprentice learns directly from a skilled teacher who helps him or her master their trade.

- The mentor must possess a willingness to share knowledge, skills, and expertise and takes a personal interest in his or her apprentice, developing a relationship of trust.

- The mentor must be capable of providing guidance, encouragement, correction, and constructive feedback.

- The mentor shares personal wisdom, tips, strategies, approaches, experiences, stories, insights, mistakes, and successes and introduces the apprentice to other colleagues who can be of assistance.

- The mentor is not someone with all the answers but is a facilitator of learning and growth.

- The apprentice is ultimately responsible for his or her own growth.

Faith formation needs to take on the look and feel of a mentor-apprentice relationship rather than a teacher-student relationship if we hope to prepare the hearts of those in our care. And that apprenticeship needs to be focused not so much on ministry (which is designed to build up the church) as on the apostolate (which is designed to transform the world). Our job is not to create mini clerics but rather to empower people to live out their baptism and transform the temporal order. Our goal is not to get them more involved in the parish but rather to get them more involved in the world, while leading them to see that such works flow from and to the Eucharist and the life of the parish.

> **Faith formation needs to take on the look and feel of a mentor-apprentice relationship rather than a teacher-student relationship.**

Mercy Laboratories

There is a reason that science classes are usually coupled with science labs: in a laboratory, students experience firsthand the theoretical concepts they are learning in class. This gives them an opportunity to verify for themselves the ideas they're learning. By seeing, handling,

"This is what I call catechesis with its shoes on!"

and manipulating various objects and materials in a lab, students more fully grasp the concepts they are learning. For disciples of Jesus, engaging in works of mercy serves as a laboratory where love of neighbor can be experienced up close and in depth. Here are some of the myriad ways that followers of Jesus can "experiment" with the corporal works of mercy. Be sure to instruct children to be accompanied and supervised by parents or other trusted adults when engaging in works of mercy that bring them into direct contact with people in need.

➕ **Feed the hungry.** Support and volunteer for food pantries, soup kitchens, and agencies that feed the hungry; make a few sandwiches or carry snack bars to hand out as you drive or walk through areas where you might encounter people in need; educate yourself about world hunger; avoid wasting food; share your meals with others.

➕ **Shelter the homeless.** Help neighbors care for their homes and do repairs; support and/or volunteer at a homeless shelter; support and/or volunteer for charitable agencies who care for the homeless, build homes, and provide support in the wake of natural disasters; advocate for public policies and legislation that provide housing for low-income people; consider becoming a foster parent.

➕ **Clothe the naked.** Go through your drawers and closets and find good-condition clothes and shoes to donate to agencies that provide assistance for those in need; participate in programs that provide towels and linens for hospitals in distressed areas; organize a clothing drive.

➕ **Visit the sick.** Spend quality time with those who are sick or homebound; take the time to call or send a card or an e-mail to someone who is sick; volunteer to drive patients to medical appointments and treatment facilities; volunteer at a hospital; assist those who are full-time caregivers for family members; cook and deliver meals to the sick and homebound.

➕ **Visit the imprisoned.** Support and/or participate in ministries to those who are incarcerated; support programs sponsored by agencies that advocate on behalf of those who are unjustly imprisoned; support job training and educational programs designed to rehabilitate prisoners; pray for the families of inmates; support programs that provide holiday gifts for prisoners and their families; support efforts that seek the abolition of the death penalty.

➕ **Give to those who have been made poor.** Take some small bills or loose change (or coupon books if you prefer not to carry cash) with you to hand out to people you encounter who are in need; throw your coin change into a jar and periodically donate it to a charity; if possible make a regular monetary donation to a charity that tends to the needs of those who have been made poor.

➕ **Bury the dead.** Be faithful about attending wakes and visitations; support or volunteer at a hospice; participate in a bereavement ministry; spend time with widows and widowers; take friends and relatives to visit the cemetery; support ministries that offer free Christian burials to those unable to afford one; offer daily prayers for those with terminal illnesses and for those who have died; send Mass cards to families of those who have died, volunteer at funeral luncheons.

All these are concrete, practical ways of practicing selfless love—sacrificial love, the kind of love that is the very essence of God. They are all examples of a "call to action"—something we earlier said marketers include in websites and emails to move people to take the next step (for example, "download now"). These Catholic calls to action are ways in which we find ourselves

> We find ourselves by losing ourselves.

by losing ourselves. They are all ways in which we gain life by laying down our life for others. And they MUST become an integral part of the curriculum of faith formation for all ages if we are to prepare hearts and minds.

True Tales

An interesting thing happened when I took those sixth graders to the Ronald McDonald House for their service/mercy experience (see p. 40–41). Because we were limited in the number of volunteers we could bring in, I was unable to invite the parents to join us for the experience. However, I was in communication with the parents leading up to the event because they needed to help their child prepare a dish to bring and needed to drop them off at the Ronald McDonald House. I waited outside to greet the volunteers as they were being dropped off. About half of the parents asked if they could come in and help! I was disappointed to turn them away because of the limitations placed on us, but it occurred to me that on no other evening of religious education class did a parent ask if they could come in and help! Why is this? Simply because parents don't think of themselves as being equipped to step into the role of a teacher. However, they know what it means to lay their lives down for others because they do it every day—it is second nature to them. And for that reason, they expressed a desire to help. This tells me that when it comes to evangelizing adults, we shouldn't always think of a class or a program to invite them to. Instead, we should consider inviting them to do something they feel very skilled at: laying down their lives for others.

Questions for Reflection and Discussion

> Think of an ad that makes a counter-intuitive claim (defies logic). Why are such claims effective in advertising?
> What does it mean to say that the central claim of Christianity (the paschal mystery) is counterintuitive?
> Who has laid down their life for you? For whom do you lay down your life?
> What significant service/mercy experiences have you had in your own faith formation? How have these affected you?
> How would you define or characterize sacrificial love? What does it mean to refer to God's love as agape love?
> Who has served as a mentor for you, and in what area? In what ways have you ever been apprenticed?
> How are the corporal works of mercy like a laboratory experience for those in faith formation?
> How can service/mercy experiences prepare hearts and minds in a way that book-learning cannot?

Scripture

My command is this: Love each other as I have loved you. Greater love has no one than this: to lay down one's life for one's friends.   JOHN 15:12–13

Prayer

Merciful God, thank you for all the people who have laid down their lives for me, putting their own needs aside to tend to mine. Help me now to do the same for others and to inspire those I teach to do the same. Amen.

Chapter 5

Proclaim the Resurrection as the Cause of Our Joy

One of the most often-used phrases in TV commercials is, "But wait, there's more!" Just when you think you've heard it all and that it can't get any better, the seller doubles down and tells you that it's about to get even better—beyond your wildest dreams! ("Order now and get a second set free!")

But Wait, There's More!

In our proclamation of the gospel, we have a "But wait, there's more!" moment: the Resurrection of Jesus Christ!

Just when you thought you've heard everything there is to hear about Jesus—his teachings, his miracles, his healings, and his laying down his life for us by dying on the cross—we hear the Good News that he is risen! Sin and death have been conquered once and for all. And if God can overcome sin and death, he can overcome anything, so we have nothing to fear and every reason to be joyful! In fact, the Resurrection of Jesus is not just one of many important details about Jesus Christ: it is the central and defining aspect of Jesus' identity. The Resurrection is the reason Christianity "happened." It is the cornerstone of our faith that Jesus Christ "suffered death and was buried and rose again on the third day" and it is our job as catechists to make this (and him!) known to others.

"With all his disciples coming around, I finally got smart and made a sign."

The Resurrection is the linchpin to evangelizing catechesis because it is the linchpin to the new dimension of life that Jesus Christ opened to us: eternal life—not to be reduced to or equated with "the afterlife' but with a new way of being human *now* through sharing in the divine life of the risen Christ. St. Paul stated firmly that, "If Christ has not been raised, our preaching is useless and so is your faith" (1 Corinthians 15:14).

> The Resurrection of Jesus is not just one of many important details about Jesus Christ: it is the central and defining aspect of Jesus' identity.

So, what does it mean for us to proclaim the risen Lord? Let's look at several important aspects of proclaiming the risen Christ to others.

Proclaiming a Person

To proclaim the risen Lord means, first of all, that we proclaim a person, not a set of beliefs, not a memory, not a history lesson, but a living person with whom we are invited to enter into relationship. We can teach great lessons about historical figures such as Abraham Lincoln and Dr. Martin Luther King Jr. However, we do not proclaim that such figures defeated death and live on in glorified bodies that enable them to continue to be present with us in a mysterious way. When we proclaim the risen Christ, we are proclaiming a living person who is present to us, albeit mysteriously, and who invites us into an intimate relationship. And the Christ we proclaim is always the risen Christ. I once was in discussion with a catechist who was making plans for her catechetical year, and she said she was going to introduce Jesus chronologically so that her students encountered Jesus as the apostles did before the Resurrection. I reminded her that, while the apostles did indeed encounter Jesus before the Resurrection, it was the Resurrection that compelled them to go forth and proclaim about the person they had spent three years with. The gospel has always been proclaimed through the lens of the Resurrection, and the person we proclaim is always the risen Christ.

Facilitating Encounters with Jesus

To proclaim the risen Lord requires that we take time in our catechesis to invite learners to encounter and talk with him through experiences of reflective prayer. Too often, we teach as though we invite Jesus into the room and then make him sit in the corner while we talk about him! This turns him into a subject, and catechists do not teach a subject, but rather facilitate encounters with Christ. Experiences of reflective prayer in which people are led into a dialogue with Jesus serve to loosen the compacted soil of people's hearts and minds—something that can be achieved only through relationships. People often ask just what reflective prayer looks like. I thought it would be helpful to share an example. The following guided reflection is adapted from *Finding God: Our Response to God's Gifts*, Grade 5 (Loyola Press) on the theme of "Called to Holiness" (Time: approximately 10 minutes):

> **Too often, we teach as though we invite Jesus into the room and then make him sit in the corner while we talk about him!**

We all have imagination. Imagination allows us to go places and to do things that might otherwise be impossible. Today we are going to use imagination to help us pray. (Pause.) Now before we begin, find a position that feels most comfortable to you. (Pause.) If you like, close your eyes. (Pause.) Now relax your entire body—your neck . . . your shoulders . . . your arms . . . your legs. (Pause.) Feel all the tension flowing out of your body, into the air and away. (Pause.) Now be very still and listen to the rhythm of your breathing. Listen. (Pause.) Feel your breath go in and out, in and out, in and out. (Pause.) Now let's begin. (Pause.)

In your imagination see yourself in a place where you'd like to be. Maybe it's a place where you've met Jesus before, maybe it's a different one. You choose, because anything is possible in imagination. Why not make it your favorite time of year? (Pause.) Make the weather suit you today. (Pause.) Be there in your imagination. Wait for Jesus to join you. (Pause.)

He does almost right away. As he comes in sight, you go to meet him. He's obviously glad to see you. Hear him tell you how glad he is to be with you again. (Pause.) As usual, he asks you what you were just doing. Sometimes your answer to that question would be, "Not much." But today it's different. He asks if you've been thinking about a verse from the Bible: "For I, the

(continued on next page)

LORD, am your God; and you shall make and keep yourselves holy because I am holy."*

Now that's not your usual line of thought. But there's something in this verse that puzzles you. You don't have trouble with the idea of God being holy. But the idea of you being holy, of making and keeping yourself holy, well that needs a little more explanation. Perhaps Jesus asks you to think of qualities that you would use to describe God—maybe qualities such as loving, forgiving, patient, understanding, generous, and so on. Let's call these "God qualities." Then he asks you to think of someone you know who has some God qualities. Who is it? Tell Jesus about this person. (Pause.)

Jesus, a great storyteller himself, might ask you to share a story about this person. It may take some time to choose just one story, but that's OK. Take the time to remember and then share your story with Jesus. (Pause.)

Jesus explains that God is all-holy. He tells you that you are holy when you act in a God-like manner. When you live your life with generosity, understanding, patience, then you are holy. Yes, you! You are holy. What an awesome statement. Now think about that. (Pause.) Do you tell Jesus that being holy is what you want, but you're a little bit worried about being able to live up to that calling? (Pause.)

As usual, Jesus is reassuring. He wants you to know that you don't become holy all at once. You grow in holiness. You'll make mistakes but that's OK. You can always learn from them and try again. He reminds you that the Holy Spirit is always with you to guide you. Jesus says that he himself will help you anytime you need him. (Pause.) Does that make you feel better? (Pause.) Go with Jesus now deep down into your heart. You've discussed a lot with him already, so now just rest in his love. Words are no longer needed. Be still together. Know how much he cares for you. (Pause.)

You recognize that it's time to go now. If you want a special blessing from Jesus, just ask for it. Remember to thank him, and then say good-bye. (Pause.) Gradually bring yourself back to the room. (Pause.) Straighten up. (Pause.) Stretch. (Pause.) Plant your feet firmly on the floor. (Pause.) Look all around you. (Pause.) Everyone's here. We're all back.

* Scripture citation in this reflection is Leviticus 11:44

Proclaiming with Joy

To proclaim the risen Lord requires that we *always* proclaim with joy! This is not to be confused with "putting on a happy face" or being glib. When we evangelize, we lead, not with doctrine or morality but with an attitude of joy. We can compare this to teaching someone the love of the game of baseball, something that we don't accomplish by handing them a rule book. We teach the love of the game by inviting them to play baseball and experience the joy of the game. *Then* we teach them the rules. In the same way, we don't make disciples of Christ by debating people, lecturing them, or bombarding them with apologetics. We do so by inviting them to experience the joy of encountering the risen Christ.

> To proclaim the risen Lord requires that we always proclaim with joy!

One of the first and most important ways that we express joy to others is through our hospitality: our way of telling others that this will be an encounter of joy and that their presence is adding to that joy. Few things create a sense of joy as much as someone showing delight in your presence. Children constantly seek the attention of their parents, begging them to look at them as they do something creative. When their parents' gaze falls upon them with delight, they experience a sense of joy. Even as adults, when someone greets us with delight, our sense of joy increases.

> God speaks in the silence of the heart, and we listen. And then we speak to God from the fullness of our heart, and God listens. And this listening and this speaking is what prayer is meant to be.
> —St. Mother Teresa of Calcutta

Think of how God the Father spoke words of delight in his Son, Jesus, when he emerged from the waters of the Jordan after being baptized by John: "This is my Son, whom I love; with him I am well pleased" (Matthew 3:17). There is no greater blessing than knowing that your parents delight in you. When we, as catechists and ministers of the church, show delight in others, we are expressing the delight that God has for them. Hospitality is one of the ways we extend God's blessing to those we encounter and should never be underestimated as an evangelizing tool. It is, in fact, one of

As part of his plans to make the parish more welcoming and hospitable, a pastor recruited a corps of greeters to welcome people at Sunday Mass and other parish events. While the new ministry was successful, the pastor was concerned about one greeter, a retired parishioner named Charlie, who always arrived late. Even though he was tidy, clean shaven, well-dressed, polite, and welcoming, Charlie was always ten or fifteen minutes late for parish events. Not wanting to dismiss Charlie outright, the pastor decided to have a chat with him, saying, "Charlie, you're a wonderful greeter, but you're always late. Have you always had this problem?" Charlie responded, "I suppose I have." Thinking he could gain some insight for how to proceed, the pastor asked, "How did they respond when you showed up late for work?" Charlie shrugged and said, "Nothing extraordinary. They would jump up, salute, say, 'Good morning, General' and ask if I wanted coffee or tea."

THE most important evangelizing tools we have, so critical that the U.S. Bishops identified it as the second of three goals in their evangelization document *Go and Make Disciples*:

> Goal II: To invite all people in the United States, whatever their social or cultural background, to hear the message of salvation in Jesus Christ so they may come to join us in the fullness of the Catholic faith.

The following paragraphs of the document go on to talk about how that invitation must be characterized by a welcoming spirit that enables people to "feel at home" and that in order to achieve that goal, we must conduct a "review of the hospitality of our institutions." As catechists, that begins with us and our own settings.

Joy is an essential nutrient in the soil of our lives if the word of God is to take root. While anger and despair compact the soil, joy loosens it up. As catechists, we play an enormous role in the spreading of joy. Albert Einstein insisted that "it is the supreme art of the teacher to awaken joy in creative expression and knowledge." The joy that we spread is not superficial: it is grounded in our belief that the risen Christ is among us and the power of the Resurrection is shared with us. In my book *Under the Influence of Jesus*, I explained,

Creating a Climate of Joy

There are several ways that we can and must create a climate of joy for those we encounter:

> The physical setting should express joy for those who enter and should communicate that "something wonderful is about to happen here and I/we were eagerly awaiting you."

> The way people are greeted and welcomed communicates joy at their arrival.

> When possible and allowed, refreshments can significantly add to the sense of joy and welcome.

> Other elements that add to the joy of any gathering include art, visuals, smiles, humor and laughter, music and singing, and playfulness.

Happiness and joy are not the same thing. Kingdom-dwellers are not people who put on rose-colored glasses and flippantly sing, "Don't worry; be happy!" No, kingdom-dwellers are filled with a deep and limitless joy, one that bears little resemblance to fleeting euphoria. This joy is a pervasive, abiding gladness, an inner peace that flows from being secure in God's love. And nothing makes us more joyful and secure than the knowledge that Jesus Christ is risen and will come again! As a result, joy is capable of withstanding anything that life tosses its way, even suffering.

Joy is something we experience when we recognize our own well-being, which is why St. Ignatius of Loyola recommended the daily *examen* as a way of calling to mind all for which we are grateful. An attitude of gratitude cannot help but be joyful as well.

> St. Ignatius of Loyola recommended the daily *examen* as a way of calling to mind all for which we are grateful.

The Art of Accompaniment

Finally, to proclaim the risen Christ means that we accompany people who are not experiencing joy but are mired in despair. Our presence alone is the assurance that joy will return; we need not engage in happy talk as much as we need to offer simple presence and reassurance. As author and scholar N.T. Wright explains, because of the Resurrection, "A new power is let loose in the world, the power to remake what was broken, to heal what was diseased, to restore what was lost" (*Simply Jesus*). To proclaim the risen Christ means to always be proclaiming a future of hope—not of doom and gloom—because the Resurrection of Jesus Christ indicates what is in store for us if we remain faithful. To proclaim the risen Christ means to teach and practice mercy, because the risen Christ returned, not for revenge against those who betrayed him, but to extend mercy and forgiveness. Followers of Jesus proclaim joy not only through words but also through actions, primarily the spiritual works of mercy:

➕ **Instructing:** deepening and sharing your understanding of the faith with others; sharing your insights, knowledge, and skills with others, especially coworkers; taking time to tutor those who are just beginning tasks such as parenting or a new job; reading inspirational literature and encouraging others to do the same.

➕ **Advising:** being courageous yet compassionate in calling people and institutions to be faithful to gospel values; intervening in situations in which people are clearly doing harm to themselves or others; responding to negative and prejudicial comments with positive statements; putting an end to gossip by walking away; setting a good example for others.

➕ **Consoling:** working at being optimistic and avoiding cynicism; responding to cynicism, skepticism, and doubt with hope; being articulate about your own hopes; asking people about their hopes and supporting them in their trying to attain them.

> We need a church capable of walking at people's side, of doing more than simply listening to them; a church which accompanies them on their journey."
> —POPE FRANCIS

➕ **Comforting:** walking with others through their pain; offering words of encouragement to those who seem discouraged; offering positive words to coworkers who are having a difficult time with their tasks; being present to those who are struggling or in emotional pain or despair; offering sympathy to those who are grieving.

➕ **Forgiving:** praying for those who have wronged you and praying for the courage to forgive; asking forgiveness from others; letting go of grudges; going out of your way to be positive with someone you are having a difficult time with.

➕ **Bearing wrongs patiently:** working at being less critical of others; overlooking minor flaws and mistakes; giving people the benefit of the doubt; assuming that people who may have hurt you did so because they are enduring pain of their own; praying for those who have wronged you.

Remember, the Resurrection is the reason Christianity "happened." So, let's proclaim the risen Christ and spread the joy of the Resurrection to a world that is desperately in need of new life.

> **Remember, the Resurrection is the reason Christianity "happened."**

True Tales

Once, when I was teaching a catechist formation course on prayer, I introduced the concept of leading guided reflections to the catechists in my group. Some had done guided reflections before, but most had not, and they were very interested in the concept. One catechist was extremely excited about the possibility of leading young people in guided reflections and insisted that she would try it out that coming weekend and would let us know how things went at our session the following week.

Sure enough, when next week rolled around, she couldn't wait to tell her story.

I serve primarily as a substitute catechist, so this past weekend I was asked to sub for a fifth-grade class. When I went into the room and started to get ready to begin, a boy came up to me and asked, "Who are you?" I told him my name and that I was the substitute for this class. He responded, "That's fine, but you need to know that I don't believe in God." I was taken aback but decided not to get into it at that moment, so I thanked him for sharing that information and asked him to take his seat and to join in the proceedings. I kept an eye on him as I talked about the importance of having conversations with God, especially about what we are thankful for. I asked each child to name one thing they were thankful for, and he did indeed offer up one thing for which he was thankful.

Then, I invited them to close their eyes, and I led them in a guided reflection where they spoke silently to Jesus about what they were thankful for and listened to Jesus respond to them. Again, I kept an eye on the boy, and he continued to cooperate and participate. After class, I noticed that the boy lingered. Eventually, he came up to me and asked, "Are you going to be here next week?" I told him that I was indeed. "Good," he replied. "Are we going to do that prayer thing again?" he asked. When I told him that we would, he again replied, "Good," and he departed. I felt that the Holy Spirit guided me to respond to his claim of unbelief, not by engaging him in debate but instead by helping him encounter God in prayer. Instead of aiming at his head, I think I touched his heart.

To that, I say, Amen!

Questions for Reflection and Discussion

> Think of the last TV commercial you saw that included the phrase, "But wait, there's more!" What was the "more" that was being promised?

> How is the Resurrection our "But wait, there's more" moment in our proclamation of the gospel?

> "Resurrection is the reason Christianity "happened." Explain this in your own words. Why do we consider the Resurrection the linchpin of our proclamation of the gospel?

> How is proclaiming the gospel different from teaching about historical figures such as Abraham Lincoln or Martin Luther King Jr.?

> How do you or can you help those you teach to encounter the risen Christ in your faith formation sessions?

> In what ways do you communicate joy to those you teach? What can you do to foster a climate of joy in your faith-formation setting?

> Describe an experience in which you were welcomed by someone with delight. What does it mean to you to be welcomed in this way? How do you welcome others?

> What is the difference between joy and happiness? How is joy proclaimed by being present to others?

Scripture

I have told you this so that my joy may be in you and that your joy may be complete. JOHN 15:11

Prayer

Risen Lord, fill me with the joy of your Resurrection. Help me proclaim that your victory over sin and death means that your grace can overcome any obstacle. Inspire me to share that joy with others, especially those overcome by despair. Help me to joyfully accompany your people. Amen.

Chapter 6

Extend Invitations to Follow Jesus More Closely

Ultimately, a TV commercial is an invitation: after presenting all the information about their amazing product or service, the sponsors invite potential customers to join other satisfied customers. They then provide a phone number, a website, and convenient locations so that potential customers can avoid being left out. In a similar manner, an effective website or marketing email always includes what is referred to as a CTA—a call to action that usually takes the form of a "button" or hyperlinked line of text that invites you to learn more, buy now, get fifty percent off, or download now, just to name a few.

Don't Be Left Out

Throughout the Old Testament, we find God constantly inviting his people to draw near to him. Few invitations are more eloquent and inviting than the Great Invitation of Isaiah 55:1–3:

> **Throughout the Old Testament, we find God constantly inviting his people to draw near to him.**

> Come, all you who are thirsty,
>   come to the waters;
> and you who have no money,
>   come, buy and eat!
> Come, buy wine and milk
>   without money and without cost.
> Why spend money on what is not bread,
>   and your labor on what does not satisfy?

Listen, listen to me, and eat what is good,
and you will delight in the richest of fare.
Give ear and come to me;
listen, that you may live.
I will make an everlasting covenant with you,
my faithful love promised to David.

Likewise, at the heart of Jesus' message is an invitation to a whole new way of being human. In fact, the gospels tell us that Jesus was constantly inviting people to follow him:

> **The gospels tell us that Jesus was constantly inviting people to follow him.**

- ➕ "Come and have breakfast." (John 21:12)
- ➕ "Come, follow me, and I will send you out to fish for people." (Matthew 4:19)
- ➕ "Go, sell everything you have . . . Then com, follow me." (Mark 10:21)
- ➕ "Come to me, all you who are weary . . . and I will give you rest." (Matthew 11:28)
- ➕ "Come, and you will see." (John 1:39)
- ➕ "Follow me." (John 1:43)

Invitations Loosen the Soil

In a general sense, our catechesis is an invitation to follow Jesus. However, evangelizing catechists take it a step further and issue specific invitations for those they teach to deepen their commitment to Christ. Some examples might include invitations to

Passing Along the Invitation

It's important to note that upon accepting Jesus' invitation, Andrew and Philip immediately proceed to extend the invitation to others: Andrew to his brother Simon Peter (John 1:41) and Philip to Nathaniel (John 1:46). Pope Paul VI famously wrote, "It is unthinkable that a person should accept the Word and give himself to the kingdom without becoming a person who bears witness to it and proclaims it in his turn." (*Evangelii Nuntiandi*, 24)

- participate in a retreat experience;
- engage in service/works of mercy;
- collaborate on a project;
- participate in a liturgical ministry such as lector, altar server, cantor, usher/greeter, or extraordinary minister of Holy Communion;
- join a faith-sharing/Bible study group or some other small-group experience;
- become a leader of a small group or serve as an aide;
- attend a workshop, seminar, rally, or conference to hear an inspirational speaker.

Invitations to new experiences serve to loosen the soil of people's lives, helping them get out of the rut of compacted soil that is holding them back.

> **Invitations to new experiences serve to loosen the soil of people's lives – helping them to get out of the rut of compacted soil that is holding them back.**

Permit me to share an example of an invitation I received as an adolescent that had a profound impact on my life. When I was in high school, I took up playing guitar, determined to be a rock star! My chemistry teacher, Father Terry Baum, SJ, took notice and invited me to accompany him at our school liturgies at St. Ignatius College Prep. I had no particular interest in liturgical music, but I thought Father Terry was pretty cool, and so I accepted his invitation.

The experience of playing at these liturgies had a major impact on me. In no time, I got in touch with the coordinator of music at my parish and joined the guitar choir to play at Sunday Mass. It just so happens that, through this experience, I started dating one of the other guitarists in the group, a young lady named Joanne, who would eventually become my wife! While I never became a rock star, I did become liturgy director at the high school where I taught and later at the parish where I served as DRE. One small invitation can make a huge difference in the life of a young person!

I didn't realize it at the time, but Father Terry was practicing Catholic evangelization. He wasn't asking me if I was saved, born again, or had a personal relationship with Jesus Christ. However, his invitation led to me encounter Jesus Christ and to begin developing a life-changing relationship with him.

Now It's Our Turn

In years gone by, the priests and nuns who staffed most faith-formation programs and taught in Catholic schools recognized that it was their job to invite young people to respond to the call to live out their baptism and, perhaps, to consider priesthood or religious life. Now, as the lay majority who staff faith formation programs most everywhere, it's our turn to pick up this task. As catechists and teachers, we need to be on the lookout for opportunities to invite young people to use their gifts to serve others and, in doing so, to encounter Christ and to experience a better way of being human. If we want to prepare people's hearts and minds for responding to God's word and ways, we need to invite, invite, invite.

> **If we want to loosen the soil of people's hearts and minds, we need to invite, invite, invite.**

When Inviting Young People, Proceed with Caution

When extending an invitation to anyone—especially young people—be sure that the invitation

> - is for more than one person so that one individual is not being singled out;
> - is approved by a pastoral staff member, usually the catechetical leader;
> - is issued on behalf of yourself and some other pastoral staff member;
> - is communicated to the parents of young people and requires their permission;
> - includes details and facts about the nature of the experience and safeguards that it will be in place for young people;
> - indicates to whom questions may be directed;
> - identifies other adults who will be present to supervise and/or chaperone;
> - provides the invitee with a true choice/an easy out if they prefer not to accept;
> - follows all parish and diocesan policies.

Before we go any further, however, I would be remiss if I did not share this major caveat. Times have changed since Father Terry invited me to assist him at our high school liturgies. Back then, it was perfectly acceptable for me to pick up my guitar, hop on the bus, and head down to the Jesuit residence to practice with Father Terry and one or two other classmates on a Saturday afternoon, and thankfully, everything was as innocent as it sounds. However, we have lived through a very serious breach of trust in our church—the clergy sex abuse crisis—which has radically changed how we interact with others, especially with the young. Today, we minister in a church that rightly requires safe-environment training for all its ministers, training that helps us know the difference between acceptable and unacceptable behaviors and practices so as to totally avoid situations that predators take advantage of. As a result, how we invite others to deepen their relationship with Christ is paramount, lest our actions and intentions be misinterpreted.

> True teachers use themselves as bridges over which they invite their students to cross; then, having facilitated their crossing, joyfully collapse, encouraging them to create bridges of their own.
> —Nikos Kazantzakis

Invitations Can Change Lives

Now, with that as a backdrop, let's revisit the notion of personal invitations and talk about their power. I can still recall the very first invitation I received to attend a friend's birthday party. I was in the fifth grade, and the invitation was from my classmate Frank Garcia. I was absolutely thrilled to be considered "one of the guys" (no girls at this party—none of us was interested yet!) and to hang out at Frank's house for an afternoon. Fast-forward a few more years

to my freshman year in high school and imagine how thrilled I was to be invited to spend a week at my friend Joe's summer home in Wisconsin over the summer break. I felt so honored to be invited. That week changed my life, and Joe and I are still best buddies to this day—and my wife and I now own a lake home on the same lake as Joe and his wife. Finally, it was a lunch invitation back in 2002 that led to the wonderful opportunity to join Loyola Press, where I have served since.

Think of the invitations you have received—invitations that have made a difference and perhaps even changed your life. It's possible that an invitation led to a new friendship, a new hobby, your present job or career, your significant other, or choosing to live in the part of the world you presently live in. As a catechist, you are most likely serving because of the invitation of another, whether it was the catechetical leader, the pastor, or another catechist. God tends to invite or call us through other people. As catechists, it is our responsibility to pass along God's call to those we teach.

And yes, personal invitations can change lives, because they can change the way we think and feel about ourselves and others. This means that invitations serve as a critical tool in the process of conversion, which is the call to change how we think, feel, and act. Personal invitations create an emotional connection, and this is a critical part of the whole process. It's one thing to read an announcement or receive a flier inviting us to an event. It is quite another thing to have someone tap us on the shoulder and personally invite

> **Personal invitations can change lives, because they can change the way we think and feel about ourselves and others. This means that invitations serve as a critical tool in the process of conversion.**

The Power of an Invitation

Invitations are very powerful. They make the invitee feel

> special
> affirmed
> honored
> wanted

> accepted
> noticed
> part of a relationship
> part of something bigger than ourselves

A pastor attended a catechist meeting and emphasized the need for catechists to be more inviting to young people and their families. He encouraged them to extend a dinner invitation to the families of children they teach. One curmudgeonly catechist reluctantly decided to go along and invited several families to dinner at her house. She tried to put on her best face even though she found the whole experience annoying. Once everyone settled down at the dinner table, she turned to her 6-year-old daughter and said, "Would you like to say the blessing?" "I don't know what to say," the girl replied. "Just say what you hear Mommy say," replied the catechist. Her daughter bowed her head and said: "Dear Lord, why on earth did I invite all these people to dinner?"

us to an event or experience. Such invitations often are accompanied by words of flattery, such as, "This sounds like a fun experience, and that made me think of you" or "This event attracts a lot of very talented people, and naturally I thought of you." The fact is, personal invitations continue to be at the top of the list of reasons people give for visiting a church for the first time—often ranging between 75–90 percent.

How to Spot Potentials

How do you spot "potentials"—people to whom you'd like to extend an invitation to grow? Consider the following, and think of those participants who

- show high enthusiasm and curiosity
- ask a lot of questions
- are influential and whose attendance may cause a "ripple effect"
- are just beginning to show some previously untapped potential
- have a specific talent that is suited for the event
- show sincerity and authenticity
- exhibit leadership skills and qualities
- possess values that are exemplary
- may be tempted to "go the wrong way" in their choices without guidance

When issuing invitations, however, be strategic and avoid throwing spaghetti at the wall and hoping something will stick. Make every effort to identify the qualities, talents, and characteristics of the individuals you are inviting and match them to the appropriate opportunity. Likewise, do your best not to extend invitations by text or email or even in person if on the fly. Instead, arrange to set aside time to talk. Telling someone that you would like to speak to them about something raises their curiosity and makes them feel as though you've been putting some thought into this—it didn't just occur to you in an offhand way. Also, avoid putting people on the spot and demanding an answer. Rather, lay out all the details and then give them time to think about it. Then follow up with them.

> Although I wasn't invited to shake hands with Hitler, I wasn't invited to the White House to shake hands with the President either.
>
> —Jesse Owens

The Power of "The Ask"

It's imperative that we make one very important observation about personal invitations: nothing will happen unless you personally extend the invitation! In the world of sales, this is referred to as the "power of the ask" which means that the best way to formalize a sale is to ask some variation of the question, "So, would you like to purchase?" Some salespersons can strike up a conversation, tell a great story, or express wonderful ideas, but never get around to asking the customer if they want to buy! By the same token, many people who shop online place items in their "cart" but never proceed to checkout, which is why companies with good marketing savvy remind folks that they have placed items in their cart and invite them to complete the purchase by proceeding to checkout.

The truth is, asking/inviting is not easy. We can be hesitant to ask or to invite someone because we may fear rejection, we may fear that we will be judged (based on what we are inviting them to), and we may fear that they will not value what we value and that they will trivialize or dismiss it and thus dismiss us too. When you ask or extend a personal invitation to someone, you are making yourself vulnerable, which is actually an admirable and attractive trait. At the same time, you are affirming the person to whom you are extending the invitation. The bottom line is, by asking/inviting someone, you are empowering both yourself and another person.

In the end, extending personal invitations says a lot about the inviter. To invite is to create an atmosphere of welcome, and that can go a long way toward a person eventually accepting an invitation, even if they are not ready to accept one in the present. It may also lead them to redirect the invitation to another person who they feel would be more inclined to respond affirmatively at the present time. Like John the Baptist, we must be like the one who, when he saw Jesus passing by, said to two of his disciples, "Look, the Lamb of God!" (John 1:36) Invitation is at the heart of learning. We can have all the most wonderful design, delivery systems, and assessment, but it is the power of the invitation to learn that makes all of the difference in the world and provides just one more reason no video or online resource can ever take the place of the person of the catechist who alone can communicate a personal invitation.

> **To invite is to create an atmosphere of welcome.**

> **Invitation is at the heart of learning.**

True Tales

I'd like to end this chapter with a story about how one football coach used the power of invitation to motivate his team. A friend of mine once related the story of his days on the football team at Moeller High School in Cincinnati back in the 1970s, preparing to play for the state championship. The coach of the team was a gentleman named Gerry Faust, who went on to become coach at Notre Dame and later at the University of Akron. Coach Faust was known for his high level of enthusiasm and for his gravelly voice. As the team gathered in the locker room right before taking the field, Coach Faust pointed to every player on the team and invited them, one by one, to share what they intended to do to help the team win the championship. It sounded something like this: "Tommy, you're the QB. What are you gonna do to make sure we win today? Brian, you're the running back. What are you gonna do to make sure we win today? Darnell, you're the middle linebacker. What are you gonna do to make sure we win today?" Each player responded with a strong statement of what he was going to achieve to help the team win the state championship, which they did. At the heart of this strategy was a personal invitation to each player to rise to the occasion and assume their responsibility to help carry the team. As catechists, we are responsible for coaching others so that they might recognize how God is inviting them to live out their baptism each and every day and respond to the best of their ability. We are, in essence, asking them, "What are you gonna do today to live as a disciple of Jesus Christ?" And then, like any good coach, we show them the "x's and o's" that enable them to succeed.

Questions for Reflection and Discussion

> Recall the first invitation you received to a party as a child. How did it make you feel to receive this invitation, and why was it so important to you?

> What was an invitation that led to a major change or decision in your life such as career, spouse, living location, or hobby?

> What power does an invitation have? In other words, what does an invitation do to the invitee?

> What are examples of Jesus personally inviting others to follow him?

> Who invited you to participate in your present ministry(or ministries)? Who have you invited to ministry?

> What are some of the things we need to keep in mind when extending invitations, especially to young people, to ensure a safe environment and avoid having our intentions misinterpreted?

> Who are some of the potentials we should be seeking to extend invitations to for deeper growth?

> Why are we often afraid or hesitant to extend invitations to others? How can we overcome this?

Scripture

Come and see what God has done,
his awesome deeds for mankind!
He turned the sea into dry land,
they passed through the waters on foot—
come, let us rejoice in him.
Psalm 66:5–6

Prayer

Good and gracious God, you bless us with such abundant graces! I am forever grateful. Fill me with the courage to invite others to "come and see" the works you do so that they may come to know you and live in your loving embrace. Amen.

Chapter 7

Aim for the Heart

In his research about why some things go viral on social media, author Jonah Berger discovered that one of the main reasons is that the shared item provokes emotion, whether good or bad. Think about it: if you had a nickel for each post you've seen about a cute kitten, you'd be rich! People share things that make others smile or reach for a tissue. By the same token, negative emotions can result in sharing, such as when a news item about an injustice provokes outrage and calls people to action.

Provoking Emotion

In a similar way, people tend to select candidates to vote for based on emotion rather than on facts, issues, or policy, sometimes even subconsciously ignoring key details that conflict with their emotional stance. This, of course, explains why so many political ads are negative; they seek to provoke an emotional response, whether or not the facts add up.

The bottom line is that emotions play a key role in choices and decisions people make in all areas of life. Aware of this reality, marketers often tap into emotions in their advertising. For example, if a TV commercial makes a reference to or shows images reflecting the sacrifices made by first responders, those who are

moved by the sacrifices of these brave men and women will naturally develop an affinity for the sponsor and will be more inclined to purchase from them.

One of the reasons that our faith formation efforts are struggling is that they often ignore emotion and remain at the cerebral or intellectual level where the soil tends to be compacted by ideas, beliefs, and ideologies that have deep roots and leave little room for future growth. My friend and author Julianne Stanz is fond of reminding all of us in faith formation of an old Irish proverb: "An arrow aimed at the head will never pierce the heart." In order to entice people to consider following Jesus, we need to invite them to experience conversion, which is the letting go of old ways—something that is hastened by emotions. Conversion and repentance involve both the mind and the heart (faith formation that touches the heart but ignores the head is equally ineffective). In Scripture, we are told to "put on the mind of Christ" (1 Corinthians 2:16), but we are also told to "rend" our hearts (Joel 2:13) and to pray, "Create in me a clean heart, O God" (Psalm 51:10).

> **In order to entice people to consider following Jesus, we need to invite them to experience conversion, which is the letting go of old ways—something that is hastened by emotions.**

For our faith formation to touch the heart, it needs to be much more than indoctrination. Teaching doctrine can be successful only if the soil has been tilled, and the best way to loosen the compacted soil of people's hearts is to touch them through emotion.

The Affective Part of the Brain

In his book *What Do You Really Want? St. Ignatius Loyola and the Art of Discernment*, Jim Manney writes, "Psychologists talk about the three parts of the mind: the cognitive (reason and other mental processes), the conative (the will), and the affective (feelings and emotions). All of these are involved in the choices we make, but the engine that drives the train is the affective power. The traditional word for it is "heart."

We need to invite those we teach to experience the joy of discipleship while also deepening their capacity for empathy with those in need. I suggest the following ways that we can and should touch the hearts of those we teach and till the soil of their being.

Tell Personal Stories

We discussed the art of personal storytelling at length in Chapter 3, but it deserves more attention here in light of our discussion about tapping into people's emotions. We can help others *know* that something is important,

> The best and most beautiful things in the world cannot be seen or even touched. They must be felt with the heart.
> —HELEN KELLER

but it is much more effective to help others *feel* that something is important. Storytelling can do just that. Stories have the capacity to transport us from one reality to another and to consider possibilities. They also create empathy. Now, it's not your job to share your entire life story with those you teach or to seek attention or affirmation by sharing personal stories. Rather, it is helpful to listen for "triggers" with regard to their interests, needs, curiosities, and challenges, so that you can find stories from your personal experience to create an emo-

> We can help others know that something is important, but it is much more effective to help others feel that something is important.

tional connection. Most importantly, share stories that illustrate how faith in Jesus Christ has changed you and helped you grow.

Use Video

Not all stories need to be yours. You can find and utilize numerous video clips from a variety of sources including YouTube that tell stories that provoke emotion. One such video clip I have used to illustrate what baptism is all about is a short YouTube video (about 60 seconds) about a 10-year-old boy who, on Christmas morning, unwraps a present from his adoptive parents that turns out to be the framed certificate that shows that his adoption is complete and official. The boy first breaks into a huge smile as he soaks in the words of the certificate. His adoptive mother asks, "Can you read it?" and he nods his head. She asks, "Out loud?" and he shakes his head and begins to cry tears of joy. He then stands up and throws himself into his adoptive parents' arms, sobbing uncontrollably. The video illustrates the power of the symbolic act of adoption: it expresses and makes manifest a bond of love that cannot be broken. As a result, the video helps explain what St. Paul means when he talks about us becoming adopted children of God through baptism (Romans 8:15) and it helps learners "feel" what baptism is all about. Many such brief, real-life videos can provoke emotion and illustrate both the profundity and relevance of various doctrinal concepts we are proposing.

Make Good Eye Contact

All good public speakers know that, if you want to truly connect with someone, you need to make direct eye contact with them. This can be especially effective when storytelling. Whenever you reach parts of a story that are especially charged with emotion, lock in on the eyes of those you are speaking to and hold their gazes for a moment to make that personal connection and to raise the intensity of your story. Think for a moment about the power of eye contact. People use the expression "love at first sight" and, while that may sound cliché, many relationships begin with people making eye contact. When people make eye contact with us, it reveals that they are aware of us and it raises the intensity of

> Direct eye contact communicates that someone finds us fascinating, engaging, or appealing. It communicates recognition and connection.

Look Me in the Eye

Few things are more frustrating than having someone look away while you are telling them something important. In fact, one health care organization discovered that 90 percent of its complaint letters mentioned poor doctor eye contact in the same breath as an uncaring attitude. Of course, eye contact that's too intense might make people uncomfortable, so be sure not to overdo it; there is a difference between direct eye contact and staring.

the moment, making us more self-conscious and aware of our own emotions at the moment. Direct eye contact communicates that someone finds us fascinating, engaging, or appealing. It communicates recognition and connection. Direct eye contact increases people's rate of retention.

Incorporate You-Focused Language

When seeking to avoid or resolve conflict, we are encouraged to use "I-focused" language that does not blame or point fingers at others. A very effective way to make an emotional connection with those you're speaking to is to incorporate a lot of "you-focused" language in your delivery—language that makes it clear that you are speaking directly to someone. So, while it's good to share personal stories, it is important to not make it all about you. The key is to communicate that the focus is on those to whom you are speaking, which creates empathy. For example, when I was teaching eighth graders at a parish on the South Side of Chicago (predominantly Caucasian) and preparing them for confirmation, I said to them, "You know that in a few short years, most of you are going to be minorities." When they appeared perplexed, I said, "Chicago is a very Catholic city and the South Side of the city is especially Catholic. But in just over four years, most of you will be going away to college, and the fact is, Catholics are a minority in this country. Will you be ready to explain your Catholic faith to those who ask?" It made for some very good conversation and laid the foundation for convincing them that paying attention to Mr. Paprocki just might be worth their while.

Use Names

Another effective tool for making an emotional connection with those to whom you are speaking is to use their names. According to a 2006 study from the Institute for the Study of Child Development, hearing one's own name significantly impacts the brain. Once, when leading a guided reflection for young people on the story of Jesus raising Lazarus from the dead, I focused on the line in which Jesus calls out in a loud voice, "Lazarus, come out!" (John 11:43). I then reflected on how Jesus calls each of us to come forth from the tomb and to experience new life. I then called each student by name: "Sean, come forth! Allison, come forth! Matt, come forth!" and so on. Personalizing the story brought it closer to their hearts and helped them consider how the gospel story speaks to them personally.

An RCIA catechist made a commitment to get to know and use the names of all the inquirers and decided to use some mnemonic devices to remember their names. When a husband and wife couple introduced themselves, the catechist made a mental note to remember their names by noting they were the same as those of two characters in a popular children's story. When the evening ended and they were saying goodbye, the catechist remarked to the couple, "Be careful going up that hill! But you must get that all the time." The couple gave a polite but puzzled smile as they went out the door but said nothing. After they left, an aide asked the catechist, "What was that all about?" "Jack and Jill. Up the hill. Remember?" said the catechist. "Yes," replied the aide, pointing at the couple, "but what does that have to do with Dick and Jane?"

Make Cultural and Ethnic Connections

I'm sure you've noticed that when politicians speak to specific groups of people, they often dress and speak in such a way as to connect with their audience. For example, in my home state of Illinois, which is rural for the most part (outside of the greater Chicago area), most politicians running for state-wide office tend to appear at campaign rallies dressed in blue jeans and flannel shirts with the sleeves rolled up so that they look like farmers even though they themselves are often multimillionaire businesspeople. Other politicians have learned how to speak Spanish so that they can connect to their growing Hispanic constituency. The bottom line is, identity is very important to people and, if you hope to make an emotional connection with them, it helps to connect with their core identity. A key part of people's core identity is their ethnicity and cultural background. If you want to make an emotional connection with those you teach, then be sure to make connections to their ethnicity.

> A key part of people's core identity is their ethnicity and cultural background.

Do People Recognize Themselves in the Story of Salvation?

When I was working in a parish that was becoming increasingly African American, we made an investment in a number of icons of saints of color and had a special blessing in church at a Sunday liturgy before installing the icons in the parish worship space. Much of the Catholicism practiced and taught in the United States until recent times has been almost exclusively European in nature while the population of Catholics in the United States has shifted to one in which people of color are soon to be the majority. If we hope to make emotional connections with those we teach, we need to be sure that all people can recognize themselves in the gospel we are proclaiming.

Make Connections to Pop Culture

When it comes to advertising, a very effective tool used by marketers is to make references to pop culture: movies, TV shows, music, fashion, games, and so on. A good way to get people talking is to get them talking about something they are already talking about! In addition to identifying emotions as one of the factors in things going viral, Jonah Berger includes what he calls *triggers* or stimuli that cause people to think of similar things. Pop culture can serve as an effective trigger or stimulus because it consists of things that are already "top of mind" for many people, and I would argue that many things in pop culture are "top of mind" precisely because they've tapped into our emotions: they provoke feelings of happiness, excitement, joy, and so on. By making connections to pop culture in your faith formation efforts, you are tapping into something people are already thinking or talking about, and this creates a connection. St. Ignatius referred to this as "entering through their door"—a strategy in teaching that taps into what is

> The heart has its reasons which reason knows not.
> —BLAISE PASCAL

already "top of mind" for the group you are addressing. Jesus was masterful at this as he tapped into images that were "top of mind" for the crowds he spoke to: fishing, shepherding, tax collecting, cooking, farming, raising and tending to family. Of course, St. Ignatius added that, while you should "enter through their door," you must be "sure to leave through your door;" once the connection is made, you move on to emphasize the main point of your teaching. Once that connection is made, however, chances are that your teaching will pop back up into your learners' heads the next time they encounter the "trigger" or the example from pop culture that you employed.

Connect Them with One Another

The emotional connections do not all have to involve you. In fact, blessed are the catechists who can create emotional connections between participants. While this cannot be forced, it can be encouraged and nurtured. Once, when I taught a sixth-grade class, I learned that the eleven students attended eight different schools. However, they had been together in religious education classes since kindergarten and had forged emotional connections with one another. They genuinely liked and cared about one another, and the catechists who taught them before I inherited them did a wonderful job of nurturing those emotional connections. At the other end of the spectrum, I once taught an eighth-grade class in which the fifteen students attended two different schools that happened to have an intense rivalry. Needless to say, the only emotional connection they shared was one of animosity and distrust. It took all I had to get them to coexist for a year! Ice breakers, mentoring relationships, pairings, buddy systems, small groups, pen pals, and cooperative learning activities can go a long way in breaking down barriers and fostering emotional connections for people of all ages.

Incorporate Music and Singing

Few things touch the heart like music and singing. While words alone can be powerful, they cannot provoke the same kind of emotion that music does. This explains why we have musicals and why a story like *The Sound of Music* speaks to generation after generation. We all know that "my

> **Few things touch the heart like music and singing.**

heart will be blessed" by the sound of music. I enjoy listening to a classic rock radio station in Chicago whose tag line is "the soundtrack of your life."

Indeed, many of the songs they play take me back to places and times in my past and provoke the emotions associated with each experience. Music and singing can give us chills, make our toes tap, put a smile on our face, and bring tears to our eyes. We often choose music to either match or to alter our mood. Music can give us voice to our thoughts and can also serve as an outlet for expressing emotions. In her article "Music is What Feelings Sound Like" (*Psychology Today*, 10/23/14), educator and author Cortney S. Warren claims that "music is a powerful vehicle for helping you become more aware and honest with yourself." One of the beauties of music and singing is that it is a shared experience, whether that sharing is restricted to listening together or manifested through joining voices with others and breaking into song. As a catechist, you can and should take advantage of every opportunity you have to integrate music and singing into your faith formation experiences to touch the hearts of those in your care.

Engage Learners in Works of Mercy That Involve Direct Contact with Others

We discussed doing service at length in Chapter 4. However, I'd like to emphasize one aspect that can make a world of difference: engaging in service that involves direct contact with other human beings. Of course, this is not always possible and, in some cases, may not be age appropriate (volunteering at a homeless shelter is typically not appropriate for young children). However, when possible, works of mercy should bring people into contact with other people and provide an opportunity to engage them.

Creating Your Go-To Playlist

Today, it is easier than ever to incorporate music into your learning setting with portable MP3 players and small but powerful Bluetooth speakers: you can create your playlist and call up music whenever you want to integrate it into your faith formation experience. Be sure to visit my blog, *Catechist's Journey* (www.catechistsjourney. com) and search for my post "I Created My Playlist of Go-To Hymns," which provides links to more than fifty songs and hymns (short and easily repeatable so you won't need printed words) that I have downloaded to my device for use in faith formation.

Many people who are in need feel isolated, and their self-value has been damaged. While it is good to offer material goods to someone in need, it is equally important to engage them with a smile and some words of greeting, acknowledgment, kindness, concern, and simple conversation. Quite often, through such encounters, we come to recognize that those in need have much to teach us. When I took those sixth graders to a Ronald McDonald House to prepare and serve meals for the guests (as I described on pg. 40–41), we made sure to encourage the young people to engage the guests in conversation. We equipped the young people with trays and pitchers of water so that they had an excuse to continually visit each table and offer to clean or pour water and, while doing so, engage in conversation, which most did. Helping those in need is admirable. Engaging those in need is transformative.

> When possible, works of mercy should bring people into contact with other people and provide an opportunity to engage them.

Create a Sense of the Sacred and Profound by Incorporating Sacramentality

For Catholics, our emotions are touched through sacramentality. Signs, symbols, rituals, movements, gestures, silence, singing—all of these can provoke emotion in ways that words alone cannot. Just think of the countless numbers of people who stand in silent awe in front of Michelangelo's *Pieta* in St. Peter's Basilica in Rome, moved by the tenderness with which Mary is depicted cradling her broken son, Jesus. We are accustomed to this language of mystery in the ways we worship as Catholics, but for some reason, when it comes to faith formation, it's as if we forget the language of mystery and attempt to form disciples strictly through words. Consider regularly incorporating each of the following elements of the language of mystery in your faith formation experiences: song, ritual, sign, symbol, silence, reverence, gesture, movement, and metaphor. While the primary language of the brain is words, the primary language of the heart is symbolic. Our Catholic sacramental sensibility recognizes that the most profound moments in life transcend words. We need a language of mystery if we hope to prepare hearts and minds to receive what God offers.

When Words Do Not Suffice

A session I once led for sixth graders took place several days after the horrendous mass shooting at Sandy Hook elementary school in Newton, Connecticut, in which twenty children and six adult staff members were killed. Not being a trained counselor, I knew better than to try to process the experience for the young people. However, I felt it was important to address it in some fashion. For a few minutes, we very simply addressed the tragedy of the situation and the feelings of sadness and anger that many were experiencing. Then I invited the children to take turns ringing a small hand chime for each of the deceased, which they did solemnly, followed by a few moments of silence after which I simply said, "Amen" and invited them to continue holding the victims and their families in prayer. To acknowledge our grief, this was much more effective than using words.

Engage Learners in Meaningful Experiences of Prayer

It is important for us to help those we teach learn prayers. However, it is equally important that we teach them how to pray in such a way as to achieve what St. Ignatius of Loyola taught: prayer that resembles one friend speaking to another. While we covered the importance of reflective prayer in Chapter 5, one more thought is needed: when we speak to our closest friends, we typically share our emotions. Prayer should be no different. Too often, prayer is approached as a sterile, intellectual acknowledgment of God's greatness, followed by some timid pleas for help. What we need to do is recapture the honesty of the Psalms, which include expressions of every emotion imaginable—from joy and happiness to anger and frustration to despair and confusion and everything in between. Reflective prayer experiences should enable people to honestly and privately share their true emotions with the Lord. In his first Homily on

> Too often, prayer is approached as a sterile, intellectual acknowledgment of God's greatness, followed by some timid pleas for help.

Prayer, St. Theophan the Recluse (nineteenth century) wrote, "When these feelings are present, our praying is prayer, and when they are absent, it is not yet prayer." Such experiences enable people to acknowledge their emotions, connect them to Jesus, and receive the grace needed to respond and move forward. In guided reflections, participants should be invited to encounter Jesus and to "check in" with him, sharing with him how they feel at the moment. The bottom line is that when we pray, we should tell God how we feel and pay attention to the feelings God leads us to experience.

> If faith formation were simply an intellectual exercise, we could provide every participant with a book or a copy of the *Catechism of the Catholic Church*, have them read and study it, and then give an exam.

If faith formation were simply an intellectual exercise, we could provide every participant with a book or a copy of the *Catechism of the Catholic Church*, have them read and study it, and then give an exam. That's not how disciples are made, however. Faith formation is not the collection of information but the embarking on a new way of being human. Such a quest requires flesh-and-blood catechists such as you to prepare the hearts of those you teach and help them become more receptive to the word of God!

Understanding Is Good. Feeling Is Better.

In the *Spiritual Exercises*, St. Ignatius teaches us to pray with our feelings and insists that engaging with our emotions is a prerequisite to healthy discernment because our emotions are a gauge to our spiritual well-being. In fact, most of the ways that St. Ignatius taught people to pray involved emotions. His premise was that understanding was good, but feeling is better. St. Ignatius believed that we need to have a passionate, heartfelt relationship with God. He also believed that God speaks to us through our feelings and used the word *consolation* to describe feelings of being closer to God (feelings of happiness, joy, and contentment) and the word *desolation* to describe feelings of being more distant from God (feelings of despair, anxiety, and sadness).

True Tales

When it comes to provoking emotions, be careful what you wish for! Emotions can be raw and can burst forth in very unexpected ways and will not always be comfortable. I remember the first time I conducted a youth ministry activity when I was but a college student myself. As I facilitated a group of a dozen or so teens in a group activity that invited each of them to share one thing about themselves that others may not know, one of the young men began to cry as he described how most others did not know how sad he sometimes felt even though he always put on a happy face. Everyone was caught off guard because this was just supposed to be an icebreaker. Unfortunately, the person caught most off guard was the facilitator: me! I was so uncomfortable seeing this young man cry and thought I could save him some embarrassment by inviting him to step out of the room with me for a few minutes to get his composure. What a mistake that was! I basically communicated to him and to the whole group that crying was not an acceptable emotion and that it should not be a part of our proceedings. Luckily, a mentor pointed that out to me immediately following the experience. Since that time, I calmly welcome tears in any gathering and tell the person, "It's ok," when they begin to apologize for crying in front of others. Through my failure, I learned that sharing tears is a gift and that it makes a gathering more sacred because it is a movement of the Holy Spirit.

Questions for Reflection and Discussion

> What is something you've seen recently on social media that you reacted to emotionally (laughed, felt sad, got angry) and felt compelled to either comment on or share?

> What does the phrase "An arrow aimed at the head will never pierce the heart" mean to you?

> Recall the last time someone's personal story moved you. In what way were you moved?

> Who do you know who makes strong eye contact? How does that create an emotional connection?

> What is an element of your ethnicity and cultural background that provokes emotion within you?

> When was a time that you connected with someone emotionally in a group setting? Describe the experience and what brought it about.

> To what extent do music and singing provoke emotions within you? What sacred image provokes emotion within you? When did performing a work of mercy provoke emotion within you?
> How comfortable are you sharing your honest feelings with God?

Scripture

Trust in the LORD with all your heart
and lean not on your own understanding.
PROVERBS 3:5

Prayer

Loving God, help me to place my trust in you with all my heart, as trust is a matter of the heart. Help me touch the hearts of those I teach with your life-giving Word, so that they might place their trust in you. Amen.

Chapter 8

Build and Deepen Commitment to a Better Way of Living

Many advertisements not only entice you to purchase a product, they also invite you to prioritize your life around an idea. Some of the best examples of this are diet plans, which are no longer just about losing a few pounds but adopting a new lifestyle. When I stroll into the kitchen at Loyola Press during lunch time, I see various coworkers meticulously preparing their dishes according to the philosophy and strategy of whatever plan they have committed to. They are not skipping meals; they are eating differently. And, to their credit, the results are often quite obvious as they appear slimmer and healthier looking over time.

Helping People to Live Differently

The invitation that we catechists offer to those we teach should follow the same approach. We are not just inviting people to stop doing sinful things. We must be about the work of helping them live differently. We are not just inviting them to "sprinkle a little Jesus" on top of their existing lives to add flavor. We are not inviting people to admire Jesus or to become a fan of Jesus. We are not inviting them to be interested in Jesus. We are inviting them to make a commitment to Jesus. We are inviting them to follow Jesus and to rely on him. To follow

"I'm all for the *concept* of conversion, as long as it doesn't require any change in my behavior."

Jesus requires that we re-prioritize our lives, adopting a new philosophy and strategy for living to create a new lifestyle—to embark upon a better way of being human.

Relationships change us. The further we pursue a relationship, the more it changes us. This is why we can often tell if someone has fallen in love or entered into an unhealthy relationship. We notice a change in the way they act, the way they look, how and where they spend their time, and who they spend their time with. Whether positive or negative, relationships change us and cause us to shift our priorities. Our goal is to invite those we teach into a relationship with Jesus—a relationship that will bring about changes in their lives and cause them to prioritize Jesus and his mission at the center of their lives.

> Relationships change us. The further we pursue a relationship, the more it changes us.

The Discipleship Diet

Changing one's lifestyle takes commitment, and we live at a time when people struggle with commitment: the act of "binding" oneself to another person, an idea, or a specific practice. Commitment is challenging because we fear getting hurt, making the wrong choice, relinquishing freedom, shifting priorities, repeating mistakes, or reliving past traumas. We also fear the emotional attachments that come with an obligation to another person or group. And that is precisely why we need to be upfront with people about how challenging a life of discipleship will be. It will take discipline, which is why, during Lent, we practice the Lenten disciplines of fasting, prayer, and almsgiving—the three main ingredients in the discipleship diet. Not everyone is up to making this commitment at the moment we propose it; just think of the rich young man who went away sad after Jesus invited him to change his lifestyle (Mark 10:17–31). The truth is, preparing our minds and hearts for discipleship is hard work.

> The truth is, preparing our minds and hearts for discipleship is hard work.

Discipleship is a lifestyle change that holds the promise of salvation—something that author Barbara Brown Taylor defines as "a transformed way of life in the world that is characterized by peace, meaning, and freedom"

(*Speaking of Sin*). So, what would the discipleship diet look like, and how can we empower people to make lifestyle changes as opposed to just learning a few doctrines?

Provide Support

Dieticians usually recommend that a person follows a plan and does not go it alone. In their advertisements, the Jenny Craig weight-loss program emphasizes the "power of personal support" as a constitutive part of their program (customers are assigned a personal consultant to connect with at least once a week). Most of the people I bump into in the lunchroom at work who are following specific diet plans are doing so with a spouse or a friend. The logic is that remaining faithful to a commitment stands a better chance of success when there is structure and support. In the discipleship diet, we commit to a plan and to a community that offers support—and we use the word *gospel* to refer to that plan and *church* to refer to our support system.

> To convert somebody, go and take them by the hand and guide them.
>
> THOMAS AQUINAS

In our faith formation, we tend to have structure of content, but we need to get much better at providing support that helps people to embrace and internalize the concepts we are proposing. This is not a new concept for the Catholic Church. Since the earliest times of the church, Christians have provided sponsors for Christian initiation. In recent times, however, the role of the sponsor has unfortunately devolved into a role that is primarily ceremonial. We need to retrieve the role of sponsor as a true mentor in faith formation so that newer disciples have the support of more seasoned disciples as they seek to implement the lifestyle changes that go with following Jesus. Mentors help to prepare hearts and minds. Without such support, the seeds of faith too often fall on rocky soil and do not take root.

A good example of the importance of support happened to me just a few years ago when I embarked upon a quest to learn Spanish. I signed up for a 10-week course, downloaded an app for my phone, and got to work. I made some good strides and began to acquire some Spanish phrases and increase my vocabulary. Then our instructor took ill and the course went into hiatus for a while. By the time she came back, spring weather was blooming in Chicago and my interest in going to classes waned. Within

Relational Ministry: Is There Any Other Kind?

We use the term "relational ministry" to refer to the concept that true encounters with Christ (and true transformation) must happen within the context of real relationships, not through programs alone. This means forming and fostering meaningful spiritual relationships in our ministerial setting. This is why the role of the catechist is so important: all the books, videos, websites, CDs, DVDs, bells and whistles in the entire world cannot ultimately lead to a transformative encounter with Christ unless facilitated by catechists who risk entering relationship with those they teach while also working to foster a network of relationships among those they teach.

weeks, I found that the gains I had made were quickly lost, and I could attribute that to one thing: I had no one to speak Spanish to daily. Without that support—without someone to reinforce the lifestyle change I was trying to make—my efforts were doomed. This is precisely why immersion courses are the most effective way of learning a new language.

If our faith formation efforts are going to have any hope of taking root, our learners must have regular contact with peers and mentors who speak the language of faith. We need the experience to be one of immersion in a new lifestyle. We need to marinate new disciples in the gospel of Jesus Christ and in the tradition of the Catholic Church. The best way to do that is to provide a support system of peers and mentors who interact regularly with their apprentices so that they can embrace the lifestyle changes that discipleship demands. Since the earliest years of Christianity, Christians have realized that the spiritual journey is best walked with another and not alone. In her book *The Interior Castle*, Saint Teresa of Ávila, the great sixteenth-century mystic, wrote:

> If our faith formation efforts are going to have any hope of taking root, our learners must have regular contact with peers and mentors who speak the language of faith.

It is very important for us to associate with others who are walking in the right way—not only those who are where we are in the journey, but also those who have gone farther. Those who have drawn close to God have the ability to bring us closer to him, for in a sense they take us with them.

As Catholics, we find our way to Jesus by walking with others, whether that be a group or an individual. When we make a commitment within a group, the experience not only provides support but also reinforces the notion that we are committing to something bigger than our self. On the individual level, we find support in mentors. Mentors are not experts. They are not theologians. They have not achieved some level of perfection. Mentors are simply a few steps ahead of the person they are mentoring. In the Rite of Christian Initiation for Adults RCIA, those preparing for baptism are provided a sponsor whose responsibility is "to show the candidates how to practice the Gospel in personal and social life" (RCIA 75). Just as a carpenter or a chef guides an apprentice into their craft, the spiritual mentor guides an apprentice—someone who is not as experienced—into the way of life known as discipleship.

Lay Out a Specific Plan

Diet plans identify foods and healthy eating habits that should replace the unhealthy foods and eating habits. In the discipleship diet, we commit to learning the healthy ways of thinking and acting that Jesus proposes (which is why we study Scripture and Tradition), and we commit to putting them into practice—and we use the word *penance* to describe some of these new practices, which are not punishment of ourselves but rather actions that repair us and our world spiritually. We also use the word *virtues* to refer to the healthy new ways of acting and behaving. Jesus himself connected his proclamation of the Good News to his amazing deeds of healing, restoring, and liberating: the word must be incarnated in action. There is no following the words of Jesus without following the way of Jesus.

> There is no following the words of Jesus without following the way of Jesus.

Commitment is shown through action, and if any lifestyle change is going to have any hopes for success, it needs to have a plan that involves specific and measurable actions. One of the reasons our faith-formation efforts fail is that our goals are often too vague and unmeasurable. We encourage people to be more loving, more prayerful, more charitable, more concerned for the needs of others, and so on, but we often don't provide specific action steps that can be implemented, observed, and evaluated as part of a lifestyle change. A successful diet does more than just call for

Practice Makes Catholic

Here is an example of the kinds of actions that can and should be "assigned" to those who are deepening their discipleship, above and beyond the practice of Sunday Mass attendance (that is, things that can be practiced on the other six days of the week). These can be practiced with a mentor, because they are specific and measurable.

> Incorporate sacramentals (actions and objects) into one's life and living/workspace (wear a scapular, place a crucifix or icon in a prominent location).
> Learn to pray the rosary.
> Pray the Angelus and/or the Liturgy of the Hours.
> Observe the liturgical seasons and feasts of the church year.
> Practice fasting and abstaining from meat.
> Learn devotions and approaches to prayer (the daily *examen*, *lectio divina*).
> Practice stewardship (time, talent, treasure).
> Practice the principles of Catholic social teaching.
> Learn from the lives of the saints (literature and film).
> Practice corporal and spiritual works of mercy.
> Participate in social justice efforts.
> Take to heart (learn by memory) doctrinal formulas and traditional prayers.
> Participate in a pilgrimage.
> Experience eucharistic adoration.
> Read Catholic literature.
> Read, study, and pray the Bible.
> Become familiar with Catholic hymns.
> Go on a retreat.

healthier eating: it provides specific suggestions such as a defined number of calories made up of fresh fruits, vegetables, fish, poultry, and lean proteins. It basically lays out a menu. In the same way, when it comes to our faith formation, we need to lay out a menu of specific actions that contribute to the embracing of the lifestyle change that discipleship requires.

> **In faith formation, we are very good at formulating outlines or syllabi of doctrinal topics to be addressed. What we need to get better at is developing *action* plans for discipleship.**

Project-Based Faith Formation

True commitment is all-encompassing and is characterized by the setting of priorities and goals as well as the acquisition of new skills—all of which need to be defined and laid out as a course of action. In faith formation, we are very good at formulating outlines or syllabi of doctrinal topics to be addressed. What we need to get better at is developing *action* plans for discipleship. Until we make faith formation resemble what is known as project-based learning, we stand to reap as much success as a coach would if he or she tried to teach swimming solely by way of a textbook or a lecture without having students get into the pool. Disciples need to be invited into the pool (not necessarily the deep end) and shown how to swim.

> **You can't go back and change the beginning, but you can start where you are and change the ending.**
> —C.S. Lewis

Finally, such action plans must communicate the same sense of urgency that St. Paul declared when he said, "Now is the day of salvation" (2 Corinthians 6:2) for us to get to work rearranging our lives to align with God's will. Faith formation must not be seen as a course to be completed but as an internship—an apprenticeship—into a way of life.

In project-based learning (also known as contextual education or action research), learners engage in direct experiences outside a traditional academic setting, investigating and responding to real-life challenges, questions, or problems, to develop skills, knowledge, and values while learning to take the initiative, make decisions, and be held accountable for outcomes. If we are going to build commitment within those we are forming in faith, we need to engage them in this type of active learning—in experiences that enable them to practice and reflect upon the lifestyle of discipleship rather than just learning about it passively.

This means that if participants are learning about the Beatitudes, it makes sense to have them involved in serving those who have been made poor or participating in action for social justice so they have an experience that invites them to reflect on what the phrases, "Blessed are the poor in spirit" and "Blessed are those who hunger and thirst for justice" mean. If participants are learning about the Eucharist, it makes sense to have them involved in an experience of eucharistic adoration and in feeding the hungry so that they have an experience of the real presence of Jesus in the Eucharist and in those in need. If participants are learning about the sacrament of reconciliation, they should participate in service that is restorative

Let's Be S.M.A.R.T.E.R.

Blogger Robert Kanaat emphasizes that commitment requires the setting of goals and that there is a "S.M.A.R.T.E.R." way to achieve goals. He says our goals must be:

> **Specific:** Our goals need to be quantifiable; they require clarity and precision (avoid vagueness).
> **Meaningful:** We need to have profound reasons for what we hope to do.
> **Achievable:** We need to set goals that we can actually reach (celebrate small successes).
> **Relevant:** Our goals should match our core values and what we truly want out of life.
> **Time-bound:** We need to be able to assess goals on a daily, weekly, monthly, and yearly basis.
> **Evaluated:** We run the risk of ignoring long-term goals if we don't evaluate them regularly.
> **Re-Adjusted:** If we are not reaching our goals, we need to make adjustments.

("Setting S.M.A.R.T.E.R. Goals: 7 Steps to Achieving Any Goal") in nature (for example, repairing or painting old homes or cleaning up litter in a park) so that they can experience what reconciliation is all about. Every doctrinal topic we teach can and must be connected to our life experience, and I would argue that unless we can do that, there is no good reason to teach that doctrine because doctrine is intended to help us understand life and how we encounter God in the midst of it.

Don't Ignore Sin

Diet plans typically eschew certain types of food that are deemed unhealthy, and they often go to great pains to point out how these foods cause damage, why they are so unhealthy, and what effects they have on one's body and

one's health. In the discipleship diet, we commit to avoiding thoughts and actions that are unhealthy for us spiritually, and we use the word *sin* to describe those realities. In our faith formation, we must not be afraid to address the dangers of sin. As I mentioned earlier, however, we can't simply provide a list of things to avoid. This would be no more successful than a diet plan that simply tells people to avoid meals. What is needed is an alternative

> Simply avoiding sin would also be akin to participating in a 12-step program and thinking that sobriety can be equated with abstinence from the addictive behavior.

way of eating. Simply avoiding sin would also be akin to participating in a 12-step program and thinking that sobriety can be equated with abstinence from the addictive behavior. While abstaining from the addictive behavior is the first and necessary step, sobriety involves learning a whole new way of living, thinking, and acting.

A catechist was leading the children's catechumenate and told the young people that in preparation for next week's lesson on sin, they should all read the seventeenth chapter of Mark's gospel. The following week, the catechist asked the young people how many had completed the reading assignment. All the young people raised their hands. The catechist said, "Perfect. Mark's gospel has only sixteen chapters so, let's begin our exploration of sin by looking at the sin of lying."

Focus on the Positive

As a church, we need to promote an alternative way of living. I enjoy telling people that my book *7 Keys to Spiritual Wellness* is really a book about the seven deadly sins in disguise. However, rather than focusing solely on what to avoid (something the church has done far too much of), I propose seven healthy suggestions that when practiced, serve as antidotes (or preventatives) for the deadly sins.

You may recall that the third pillar of the *Catechism of the Catholic Church* is the moral life or "life in Christ." To be a disciple of Jesus requires that we treat other people in the manner Christ has taught. This means avoiding certain behaviors (sin) while practicing other behaviors (virtues) that express respect for the dignity of others. In our faith formation, we must present virtues and virtuous behavior as the norm for the lifestyle of a disciple and we must provide opportunities, strategies, and skills for disciples to practice such behaviors to incorporate them into their lives while, at the same time, helping them identify why other actions and behaviors are unhealthy, need to be avoided, and must be guided by the Ten Commandments.

Diet plans often involve a "cleanse," which is a commitment to rid the body of toxins so that the various systems in our bodies can work more efficiently. In the discipleship diet, we commit to ridding ourselves of spiritual toxins so that our souls and spirits can thrive instead of being weighed down—and we use the words *fasting* to refer to our participation in a spiritual cleanse and *confession* and *absolution* to describe the spiritual cleanse that occurs sacramentally.

Don't Shy Away from Assessment

We said earlier that achieving goals (keeping a commitment) is more effective when it is specific, achievable, time-bound, and evaluated. For some reason, however, when it comes to faith formation, there is a tendency to shy away from "measuring" or "assessing" where disciples are in their journey. I'm not suggesting that faith formation be graded

> When it comes to faith formation, there is a tendency to shy away from "measuring" or "assessing" where disciples are in their journey.

like an academic subject. I am, however, suggesting that we need to provide methods by which we can help disciples and their mentors/sponsors discern the extent to which certain knowledge and behaviors of the lifestyle of a disciple have been embraced and integrated into daily living.

Diet plans and healthy eating/living regimens include a number of ways to determine if certain benchmarks are being achieved, including getting on a scale, calculating BMI (body mass index), taking a blood test, measuring blood pressure, recording progress in exercise, looking for evidence of healthy foods in the refrigerator and cabinets, and so on. By the same token, RCIA makes it quite clear that we—catechists and pastoral staff—have the responsibility to discern the readiness of catechumens and candidates. In talking about the Rite of Acceptance and Welcoming, paragraph 42 of the Rite explicitly states:

> The prerequisite for making this step is that the beginnings of the spiritual life and the fundamentals of Christian teachings have taken root in the candidate. There must be evidence of the first faith . . . of an initial conversion and intention to change their lives and to enter into a relationship with God in Christ.

Paragraph 43 goes on to say, "Before the Rite is celebrated, therefore, sufficient and necessary time . . . should be set aside to evaluate and, if necessary, to purify the candidates' motives and dispositions."

Finally, the Rite says that those involved "have the responsibility for judging the outward indications of such dispositions." Efforts to make this a reality in other faith formation settings have emerged to an extent in confirmation programs, taking the form of interviews with the confirmands. However, such interviews often amount to little more than an oral exam—a hoop to jump through before confirmation. Authentic assessment needs to be ongoing and multi-faceted, and parts of it should be self-assessing. Likewise, assessment should not be used as a one-time evaluation to qualify for a sacrament but should serve as a tool for determining the extent to which a developing disciple has had a conversion of heart and mind (shows a spirit of faith and charity and a desire to learn more about Jesus and the Catholic faith), has embraced new practices or actions (shows a desire to

Authentic assessment needs to be ongoing and multi-faceted, and parts of it should be self-assessing.

pray and celebrate the sacraments with the community), and has acquired new knowledge and skills to serve the mission of Christ (shows a desire to serve the mission of Christ).

The purpose of assessment in faith formation is to discern the extent to which an individual has "undergone a conversion in mind and in action and . . . developed a sufficient acquaintance with Christian teaching as well as a spirit of faith and charity" (RCIA, 120). Remember, we said earlier that when someone makes a new commitment, it is evidenced by a change in the way they act, the way they look, how and where they spend their time, and who they spend their time with. These should form the criteria for assessment in faith formation so that we can help individuals measure the extent to which they are embracing the lifestyle of discipleship.

Ritualize Every Step of Progress Made

In Alcoholics Anonymous and other twelve-step groups, it is customary to award "sobriety coins" (poker chip-sized medallions) to mark the amount of time a member has remained sober and refrained from the addiction. This ritual expresses the support and commitment of the twelve-step group to the individual and serves as motivation for the recipient to continue their quest for sobriety. Studies have shown that possession of such coins has had a positive impact on the recipient's self-resolve. That's the power of rituals and symbols. This is why the Rite of Christian Initiation for Adults is marked by rites along the journey: these rituals mark in a tangible way the progress that an individual is making on the path to deeper discipleship. This practice should be a part of all our faith-formation efforts as a way of celebrating a person's embracing of new knowledge, skills, and practices of the discipleship lifestyle. Just as the Scouts celebrate progress in experiential learning by the awarding of merit badges and awards (advancement, not competition), Catholic faith formation is perfectly suited to such ritualizing because we are a sacramental church. Prayerful rituals and outward signs (medals, holy cards, icons) can and should mark the undertaking of each new practice or period of growth (a commissioning) as well as the completion of periods of growth (not just grade levels, but more frequent) or the

> Rituals mark in a tangible way the progress that an individual is making on the path to deeper discipleship.

acquisition of new knowledge, skills, and practices that represent a deepening of discipleship.

Focus on the Why

Finally, if people are going to commit to anything, they need to know *why* they are doing it. In his book *Start with Why: How Great Leaders Inspire Everyone to Take Action*, best-selling author and speaker Simon Sinek insists that "people don't buy what you do, they buy why you do it." With nostalgia, many Catholics recall the old *Baltimore Catechism*, in which one of the first questions is, "Why did God make me?" This question and its answer—"God made me to know Him, to love Him, and to serve Him in this world, and to be happy with Him forever in heaven"—both get at the *why* of our Catholic faith. It is no coincidence, then, that the first chapter of our current *Catechism of the Catholic Church* also starts with *why*.

> The desire for God is written in the human heart, because man is created by God and for God; and God never ceases to draw man to himself. Only in God will he find the truth and happiness he never stops searching for (27).

Ultimately, people will not choose the Catholic faith and a life of discipleship based solely on what we do but also on why we do what we do. And if we understand why we do what we do, the *why* will guide what we do and how we do it!

Soil Capable of Sprouting

As evangelizing catechists, may we continue to invite emerging disciples to do more than spread a little "Jesus frosting" on the cake of their lives but rather to commit to a lifestyle change. To till the soil is literally to change the conditions in which a seed will be planted.

> **To till the soil is literally to change the conditions in which a seed will be planted.**

The work of faith formation is to help people to continually till the soil of their lives lest it become compacted and incapable of sprouting new leaves.

True Tales

I said earlier in this chapter that we need to ritualize progress that a developing disciple makes throughout the journey. The power of such

The Principle and Foundation

When St. Ignatius of Loyola wrote his *Spiritual Exercises*, he also started with *why* in what is known as the principle and foundation of the *Exercises*:

The goal of our life is to live with God forever.
God, who loves us, gave us life.
Our own response of love allows God's life
to flow into us without limit.

All the things in this world are gifts of God,
presented to us so that we can know God more easily
and make a return of love more readily.

As a result, we appreciate and use all these gifts of God
insofar as they help us develop as loving persons.
But if any of these gifts become the center of our lives,
they displace God and so hinder our growth toward our goal.

In everyday life, then, we must hold ourselves in balance
before all of these created gifts insofar as we have a choice
and are not bound by some obligation.
We should not fix our desires on health or sickness,
wealth or poverty, success or failure, a long life or short one.
For everything has the potential of calling forth in us
a deeper response to our life in God.

Our only desire and our one choice should be this:
I want and I choose what better leads to the deepening of God's life
  in me.

(*First Principle and Foundation*, as paraphrased by David L. Fleming, SJ)

rituals became evident to me many years ago when I introduced the Rite of Dismissal at Sunday Mass for our catechumens in the RCIA. I had struggled for several years with the notion of dismissing the catechumens, wrongly thinking that it was inhospitable and cruel to make them leave the celebration. After participating in an extraordinary formation experience for RCIA coordinators, however, I came to realize it was precisely the opposite: to make people stay and watch while the rest of us partake of a meal was inhospitable! So, with the proper catechesis in hand, I prepared our catechumens as well as the congregation for the introduction of the dismissal rite at Sunday Masses following the homily. The priest ritually called forth the catechumens, explained to them and the congregation what was taking place, and prayerfully dismissed them as they were led in procession to a room in the parish center by a catechist carrying the book of the Gospels as the congregation sang a refrain assuring them of their prayers. When we arrived in the parish center and settled in to break open the Word of God, I asked the catechumens what their reaction was to the dismissal rite. One of them, a very soft-spoken middle-aged African American woman, said, "I loved it. I finally felt like I knew what my role in the assembly was. Until then, I just sat there feeling lost. Now, I felt like I had an important role to play as part of the assembly." The ritual of the dismissal rite helped her solidify her deepening commitment to the Lord and to the parish community.

Questions for Reflection and Discussion

> Who is someone you know (including yourself if it applies) who has undergone a lifestyle change with regard to diet, exercise, health, and so forth? What enables someone to be successful when undertaking a lifestyle change?

> What was or is a relationship that significantly changed you and your life? In what ways?

> How does being in a relationship with Jesus and living as his disciple demand a lifestyle change?

> Who has supported you in your faith life? How did they support you? Whom have you supported, and how?

> When was a time you learned by doing? When it comes to doing the work of a disciple of Jesus Christ, what are some things you would like to be taught? What could you teach others?

> Explain the following: "Simply avoiding sin would be akin to participating in a twelve-step program and thinking that sobriety can be equated with abstinence from the addictive behavior."

> Describe a time when you and your efforts at a task were assessed and evaluated. What did you learn from that experience? How can one's development in a life of faith be assessed?

> How would you answer the following question: "Why should I consider a relationship with Jesus?"

Scripture

"For I know the plans I have for you," declares the Lord, "plans to prosper you and not to harm you, plans to give you hope and a future.
JEREMIAH 29:11

Prayer

Loving God, your plan for each of us is to prosper. Thank you for revealing your plans to us and for showing us how to fulfill them by following your Son, Jesus Christ. Help me show others the plan you have for them and help me walk with them on their journey to your embrace. Amen.

Chapter 9

Equip and Empower the Next Generation of Evangelists

Hardly anyone purchases anything online these days without first reading the customer reviews. Satisfied customers are eager to leave glowing reviews, which often include personal stories about how they have successfully used a product or resource in their unique situation in hopes that others in similar situations may benefit. Of course, disgruntled customers are just as eager to share their experiences in hopes of protecting others from making a purchasing mistake. In either case, the truth is that potential customers deeply value the experience and insights of existing customers in helping them make their purchasing decisions.

Creating a Corps of Evangelizers

In my presentations, I often tell my audiences about the book *Creating Customer Evangelists* (by Jackie Huba and Ben McConnell) not because I think they should read it, but because as Catholics, we should be aware that a book that has nothing to do with faith, religion, or spirituality, is using the word *evangelists*. The premise of the book is that customers should be so enamored with your product or service that they will not be able to resist the urge to

"Honey, I appreciate that you're taking your responsibility to evangelize our children to heart, but I think we need to talk about effective methods."

become "outspoken evangelists for your company" (as phrased in the book's description) who will spread the good word to others by word of mouth to convince them that it will be to their benefit to follow their example. Because customer evangelists are not paid but simply advocate based on their firm belief in a product or service and want others to benefit from it, they are more credible than a salesperson or professional. They are considered "evangelists" because they *believe* and they *preach*. Companies, then, are encouraged to "convert" people into "believers" who will then form a corps of evangelizers to advocate on their behalf.

I can't help but think of Jesus saying, "The people of this world are more shrewd in dealing with their own kind than are people of the light" (Luke 16:8). Is it wrong that a book on business strategies is using words such as *evangelists, conversion*, and *believers*? No. What *is* wrong is that the secular world too often does a better job than does the church in these areas! No one is going to become a customer evangelist if the product or service is mediocre: the product or service must be seen as worth spending the time to tell others about. The more a product or service is meeting a significant need of a customer, the more likely that he or she will mention it to others.

Our job, as evangelizing catechists, is to create a corps of evangelizers—people who will be so enamored with Jesus Christ and his church that they will become outspoken evangelists for his better way of being human. A Christian evangelist tends to be someone who:

> **Our job, as evangelizing catechists, is to create a corps of evangelizers.**

- ➕ seeks to encounter Jesus regularly and believes in him and is a "repeat customer;"
- ➕ can't resist offering positive comments and recommendations about following Jesus to others including family, friends, and coworkers without being asked to do so and without remuneration;
- ➕ finds ways to give the "gift of Jesus" to others;
- ➕ feels that their relationship with Jesus and the church makes them feel that they are part of something larger than themselves;
- ➕ feels a sense of connection to Jesus and the church, because they feel known, liked, cared for, and listened to.

Characteristics of Customer Evangelists

Customer evangelists typically:

> use the product or service regularly and believe in it; they are repeat customers;

> can't resist offering positive comments and recommendations to others including family; friends, and coworkers without being asked to do so and without remuneration;

> often give the product or service as a gift to others;

> feel that their use of this product or service makes them feel that they are part of something larger than themselves;

> feel a sense of connection to the company or brand; they feel known, liked, cared for, and listened to.

The first step toward making this a reality is for us catechists to stop thinking of those we teach as students and instead think of them as partners and coworkers whom we are mentoring and apprenticing. Our goal is to prepare people's hearts and minds so that they, in turn, learn how to do that for themselves and for others. We achieve this by:

> **We need to stop thinking of those we teach as students and instead think of them as partners and coworkers whom we are mentoring and apprenticing.**

⊕ not only speaking to them, but also listening to them and showing them that we truly care;

⊕ sharing "inside" information (not just doctrine but our personal stories, insights, and wisdom about living that faith in the world);

⊕ equipping them with strategies for sharing and telling their faith story and talking about their relationship

> **As iron sharpens iron, so one person sharpens another.**
> —Proverbs 27:17

with Jesus (in person as well as through social media) in a way that makes an emotional connection;

- ➕ inviting them to participate in experiences that will make them feel part of a community of like-minded people and part of a movement or a cause bigger than themselves;

- ➕ providing them with opportunities to invite others to experience what they have or what they are experiencing.

Delighting in the Success of Our Successors

For generations, parents have strived to ensure that their children will have a life that is better than their own—not just economically but also with regard to avoiding mistakes and overcoming challenges. The same is true for anyone who mentors an apprentice: we delight in their success and want to see them succeed in ways that exceed our own successes. To make that happen, a mentor does the following:

- ➕ provides the best wisdom and advice;

- ➕ shares every skill that he or she possesses;

- ➕ points out mistakes and pitfalls that need to be avoided;

- ➕ encourages the development of skills that the mentor may not possess or excel at.

As catechetical ministers who are mentoring the next generation of disciples of Christ, it is imperative that we do all the above to ensure that their proclamation of the gospel is more "effective" than our own. This book has already pointed out a number of things that the next generation of Catholics needs to be better at than previous generations: focusing on people's brokenness, establishing trust, telling stories of Jesus' mighty deeds, helping people to practice selfless love, creating a climate of joy, welcoming and inviting, touching people's hearts, and building commitment. In addition to those, however, I would like to wrap up this book by offering a few more suggestions for things that the next generation of Catholics needs to be better at than previous generations.

> **As catechetical ministers who are mentoring the next generation of disciples of Christ, it is imperative that we ensure that their proclamation of the gospel is more effective than our own.**

They will Need to Be Better at Removing the Perceived Conflict Between Science and Faith

Studies have revealed that, by age ten, young Catholics are making the decision to leave the Church, and it is typically not because they think Mass is boring. They are leaving because they are increasingly finding faith to be incompatible with what they are learning in other fields, especially science, which provide empirical evidence and proof as part of the educational process. Thus, these young people are concluding that much of what is taught in Scripture and Tradition are fairy tales that can be easily dismissed. This is unfortunate, because the church teaches that there should be no conflict between science and faith; science teaches *how* while faith teaches *why*. Science teaches that which is measurable and observable. Faith teaches about unseen realities. Thus, we say in the Nicene Creed that we believe in God, "maker of heaven and earth, of all that is visible and invisible." We believe in invisible realities that cannot be measured. As I said in my book *Living the Sacraments: Finding God at the Intersection of Heaven and Earth*:

> The more I study science, the more I believe in God.
> —ALBERT EINSTEIN

> There is much that science cannot measure or explain. Science will never be able to explain the meaning of a work of art, poetry, or literature. Science cannot define or explain beauty. Science will never be able to define goodness or joy. Science will never be able to explain the purpose of a human life. Science cannot explain what makes something funny or sad. Science cannot define what constitutes true love.

The Church teaches that there should be no conflict between science and faith; science teaches *how* while faith teaches *why*.

When it comes to teaching Scripture, the next generation will need to do a much better job of explaining that truth and fact are not the same thing and that, while everything in the Bible is *true*, not everything in the Bible is *fact*. They will need to help future Catholics resist literal interpretations of parts of the Bible (such as the stories of creation, Noah's Ark, and Jonah and the Whale) while not dismissing them as mere fairy tales because they convey essential, sacred, and—yes—divine truths. For more on this, I recommend that you reference my book *The Bible Blueprint: A Catholic's Guide to Understanding and Embracing God's Word.*

They Will Need to Be Better at Embracing Cultural Diversity

When I was growing up in St. Casimir Parish on the near West Side of Chicago, the neighborhood was changing from Polish to Hispanic. Our Polish pastor did his best to welcome the new population to the parish and even learned to speak Spanish so that on special occasions he could deliver his homilies in English, Polish, and Spanish. I recall, however, that whenever this occurred, a long-time Polish parishioner sitting in the front pew of the church would get up and loudly clomp down the long aisle in her clunky heels as soon as the Spanish segment of the homily began. When the Spanish segment ended, she would loudly return down that same long aisle for all to see and hear. It was her way of protesting the newcomers, whom she felt did not belong. While most Catholic folks do not engage

Embracing Diversity

According to CARA research, Hispanics account for 71 percent of U.S. Catholic population growth since 1960. Between 2005 and 2010, Hispanics accounted for 40 percent of the increase in registered parishioners in U.S. parishes. By the year 2030, according to Pew research, whites will no longer be a statistical majority among American Catholics, representing only 48 percent of the Catholic population while Hispanics will represent 41 percent, Asian-Americans 7.5 percent, and Africans and African Americans 3 percent. The next generation of Catholics will need to embrace and celebrate this diversity, lest non-white Catholics decide to look elsewhere for the gospel of Jesus Christ, which far too many are already doing.

in such overt actions, we need to do much more to embrace the changing faces of our parishes. I emphasize the word *embrace*—not tolerate. Diversity is to be embraced because it reflects the greatness of God and the power of God's Word to transcend all languages. Because all people are made in the image and likeness of God, people who look different from us teach us something about God that we might not otherwise recognize.

> Because all people are made in the image and likeness of God, people who look different from us teach us something about God that we might not otherwise recognize.

They Will Need to Be Better at Avoiding Political Ideologies and Focusing on Catholic Social Teaching

The next generation of Catholics must realize that we cannot be "at home" in any political party in the United States. Neither party fully embodies the teachings of the Catholic Church and we as Catholics must be seen as true independents without a blind allegiance to either party. Rather than blindly supporting one candidate or another because they fit our political ideology, we need to campaign for principles and call out any politician who is not living up to gospel principles while supporting those who are. The next generation of Catholics will need to be better at revealing one of the church's best kept secrets: Catholic Social Teaching. That this body of teaching is still considered the church's best-kept secret is scandalous at worst and an embarrassment at best. In the

> The next generation of Catholics will need to be better at revealing one of the Church's best kept secrets: Catholic Social Teaching.

parable of the Last Judgment, Jesus makes clear our responsibility to tend to the needs of others. The church teaches this responsibility in the seven principles of Catholic Social Teaching reminding us that, if we want to live as followers of Jesus, we need to live as people for others.

- ⊕ **Dignity of the Human Person.** We are called to ask whether our actions as a society respect or threaten the life and dignity of the human person.

- ⊕ **Call to Family, Community, and Participation.** We are called to support the family—the principle social institution—so that people can participate in society, build a community spirit, and promote the well-being of all.
- ⊕ **Rights and Responsibilities.** We are called to protect the rights that all people have to those things required for a decent human life, such as food, clothing, and shelter.
- ⊕ **Option for the Poor and Vulnerable.** We are called to pay special attention to the needs of those who are poor.
- ⊕ **The Dignity of Work and the Rights of Workers.** We are called to protect the basic rights of all workers: the right to engage in productive work, fair wages, private property, and the right to organize, join unions, and pursue economic opportunity.
- ⊕ **Solidarity.** We are called to recognize that, because God is our Father, we are all brothers and sisters, with the responsibility to care for one another.
- ⊕ **Care for God's Creation.** We are called to care for all that God has made.

They Will Need to Be Better at Making Faith Relevant

When St. Ignatius formed the Society of Jesus (the Jesuits) in the sixteenth century, he did something radically different from the norm: he chose not to establish a monastery, where hours would be spent in liturgical prayer. Instead, he sent the Jesuits out into the world to engage the culture and lead people to a deeper awareness of God's presence in daily life. He sought to make faith relevant to people's lives. Today, of those who self-identify as non-religious, one of the top reasons they give is that church or faith is not relevant to their lives. Ultimately, this comes down to the fact that, in every generation, young people will ask their teachers, parents, and elders the timeless question, "Why do I have to know this?" The next generation of Catholics will need to be better at answering that question ("Because I said so" will not suffice), which means that they will need to reflect deeply on the connection of every church doctrine to daily living because if a connection cannot be found, there is no reason to teach it. Everything we teach should have an if-then dynamic: "If I believe that Jesus is fully human and fully divine, then . . ." or "If I believe in the communion of saints, then . . ." And the *then* must lead to a different way of being human.

They Will Need to Be Better at Making Worship More Robust

It doesn't matter how effective our catechesis is if we, as Catholics, worship in a manner that is perfunctory and mediocre. I have heard numerous voices claim that intense apologetics will solve all the church's problems, but if the liturgy is the source and summit of the Christian life, that means that the way we worship is of the utmost importance or, as my friend Father John Breslin always reminds his congregations, "the Mass is the most important thing we do!" The Latin phrase *lex orandi, lex credendi* reminds us that the law of prayer ("the way we worship") is the law of belief

> It doesn't matter how effective our catechesis is if we, as Catholics, worship in a manner that is perfunctory and mediocre.

Keeping Ritual from Becoming Routine

There is a fine line between ritual and routine. A routine is an action we perform over and over in the same manner with *little or no thought*. A ritual is also an action that we perform over and over in the same manner with *deep and profound thought*. The next generation of Catholics will need to be better at ensuring that our liturgical rituals never become routine. They will need to ensure that our worship is always characterized by robust music and singing, robust silence, robust movement and gesture, robust homilies, robust sign and symbol, and robust rituals.

After communion at a Mass that included a very long and boring homily, the pastor announced that he wished to meet with the parish board in the sacristy following the closing song. However, the first man to arrive was a total stranger. "You must have misunderstood my announcement," said the pastor, "This is a meeting of the parish board." "I know," said the man, "but if there is anyone here more bored than I am, I'd like to meet him."

("what we believe"). This phrase is often expanded to read *lex orandi, lex credendi, lex vivendi*, which connects the way we worship with what we believe and how we live. The next generation of Catholics will need to be better at ensuring that all Catholic worship is robust and not perfunctory.

They Will Need to Be Better at Placing Expectations on Disciples

The Roman poet, Ovid, once told a story (*Metamorphoses*) of a man named Pygmalion, a sculptor who created an ivory statue representing his notion of the ideal woman. He then fell in love with the statue and prayed to the gods to give him a wife in the likeness of the statue. Aphrodite responded to his prayer, and the statue came to life and became his wife. You could say that the statue "lived up to" Pygmalion's high expectations. In education, we have the term "the Pygmalion effect," which describes the tendency of students to live up to what's expected of them and, therefore, the need for teachers to have high expectations of their students. Studies have

> The focus of faith formation should be on helping participants embrace and practice the responsibilities that are part and parcel of discipleship.

Howdy, Partner!

In my book, *A Church on the Move: 52 Ways to Get Mission and Mercy in Motion*, I wrote,

> Through the sacrament of baptism, we become partners with Jesus in his mission. We enjoy the benefits of the amazing grace that comes with partnering with Jesus, not the least of which is our salvation! At the same time, this partnership requires that we contribute to the growth of the mission that Jesus has entrusted to the church. There are two sides to the coin of discipleship. If we are going to become a church on the move, we need to pay more attention to the expectations that come with discipleship. And we can start by treating people who join our parishes as partners rather than as parishioners.

shown that teachers tend to form expectations about their students' capacity for success and then respond accordingly, treating students with "high-expectancy" differently from students with "low-expectancy." Students pick up on the differential treatment and respond accordingly. Creating a culture of high expectations is often considered an essential leadership task.

In faith formation, too often, the only expectation placed on participants is to show up and to complete the "course," usually in order to "qualify" for reception of a sacrament. Instead, the focus of faith formation should be on helping participants embrace and practice the responsibilities that are part and parcel of discipleship. When expectations run low, complacency runs high. The next generation of Catholics will need to be better at placing high expectations on those they teach so that they come to recognize themselves as partners in mission with Jesus Christ.

They Will Need to Be Better at Mastering Technology

By the time my granddaughter, Olivia, was ten months old, she could interact with a touchscreen on a smart phone or a tablet. There is no doubt that young people today are digital natives and that their exposure to and interaction with technology from the time they are very young (and their malleable brains are still developing) is "wiring" the brain to function differently from the brains of previous generations. By the time young people are engaged in formal schooling, they are accustomed to accessing information and interacting with others through digital platforms. On the day I was writing this segment, the winter weather in Chicago was brutal, resulting in school closings. However, I noticed that the scroll on the TV screen also included a number of schools declaring an "e-learning day," meaning that students did not, in fact, have a snow day but would be learning from home using technology.

For a variety of reasons, faith formation has lagged when it comes to the integration of technology in learning. Before I go any further, let me reiterate that faith formation is different from schoolwork because it is not the teaching of a subject but the facilitation of an encounter with Christ. No technology can replace the person of the catechist or mentor. At the same time, technology can provide access to learning and inspiration that supports and

> **The next generation of Catholics will need to be better at integrating the effective use of technology in the faith formation setting.**

reinforces that encounter. The next generation of Catholics will need to be better at integrating the effective use of technology in the faith-formation setting. Marshall McLuhan famously said that "the medium is the message." While that may be hyperbole, it contains a kernel of truth: the medium most definitely contributes to or detracts from the message. Without the use of current technology in their faith-formation experience, learners may easily conclude that the message we are transmitting is no longer relevant.

They Will Need to Be Better at Populating People's Imaginations with Catholic Imagery

When speaking about the roles of parents, godparents, grandparents, catechists, and teachers in forming the faith of children, my friend and colleague Tom McGrath often emphasizes the need to "populate the imaginations" of young people with stories, images, signs, and symbols of our Catholic faith. At a very young age, children develop a way of seeing the world. Some develop a positive worldview that recognizes truth, beauty, and goodness as more potent than that which is bad. Others develop a worldview that is primarily negative, seeing the world as untrustworthy and suspect. The Catholic imagination sees the world as infused with the goodness and beauty of God, and our efforts in faith formation must seek to "populate the imaginations" of young people with the stories and images of our catholic tradition.

> The Catholic imagination sees the world as infused with the goodness and beauty of God.

The imaginations of young children will be populated with something, but the question is, with what? If left up to popular culture, too many of the ideas and images that will populate their imaginations will be superficial and self-centered. The next generation of Catholics will need to be better at populating the imaginations of young people with stories (from Scripture and the lives of the Saints) and images (signs, symbols, sacramentals) that speak of a loving God who is near to us and who teaches us how to love one another as Jesus did.

They Will Need to Be Better at Teaching Prayer, Spirituality, and Discernment

When people say that they are "spiritual but not religious," they are saying that they do not find their spiritual needs being met by religious institutions. It is unfortunate that the Catholic Church is seen primarily as an institution instead of as a spiritual path. I find it interesting that when I do a Google images search for Hinduism, Judaism, or Buddhism, I find the following as the first image:

- ➕ Hinduism: an image of Krishna
- ➕ Judaism: a star of David
- ➕ Buddhism: an image of the Buddha

Yet the first image that comes up for Catholicism is a building: bricks and mortar. The next generation of Catholics will need to be better at proposing the Catholic faith as a spiritual path and the Church as being made

> The next generation of Catholics will need to be better at teaching others not just their prayers but *how* to pray.

of "living stones." In particular, the next generation of Catholics will need to be better at teaching others not just their prayers but *how* to pray. They will need to be better at presenting prayer as one of the four pillars of the Catholic faith, equal to the other three and not simply an add-on. They will need to be better at forming people in spiritual practices that nurture an intimate relationship with Jesus and make God's nearness palpable. And finally, they will need to be better at teaching the art of spiritual discernment so that disciples of Jesus turn with confidence to the Holy Spirit for help in making everyday decisions as well as major life decisions.

They Will Need to Be Better at Forming Families (Supporting Parents)

For too long, we as a church have been paying lip service to the notion that parents are the primary teachers of their children when it comes to forming them in faith and that the home is the "domestic church." And yet many, if not most, of our faith-formation models continue to encourage parents to drop off their children so that the parish can form them in faith while the parents get some errands done. In essence, we have trained parents to be very effective chauffeurs who transport their children to the parish, where others form them in the faith. In response to this unfortunate reality, Pope Francis issued a call for parents to "come out of exile" and to "reassume their educative role."

From start to finish—from the first day that parents bring their children to religious education until the day they complete their formal formation—we should be speaking to parents not about how they can pitch in to help us but how we are here to help them. It begins with the mindset that parents are going to have expectations placed on them when it comes to their children's faith formation. If that sounds heavy-handed, just stop and think of all the activities that parents enroll their children in that require parent involvement, such as taking their turn to run the hot-dog cart for the kids' soccer game. The next generation of

> **We have trained parents to be very effective chauffeurs who transport their children to the parish, where others form them in faith.**

Catholics will need to be better at both forming parents and helping the parents to form their own children. They will also need to be better at helping parents build their home into a domestic church: a place where God's presence is acknowledged, welcomed, celebrated, and responded to.

They Will Need to Be Better at Going Forth

In many medical and crime shows on TV, we encounter scenes of coroners conducting autopsies on victims to determine the cause of death. While writing this section of the book, I heard the news that several Chicago parishes are closing. What causes a parish or a church to "die"? While there are many reasons, some of them demographic, we often don't analyze the situation closely enough to prevent it from happening again. Which is why the name of a particular book caught my attention several years ago: *Autopsy of a Deceased Church: 12 Ways to Keep Your Church Alive*, by Thom Rainer. Rainer reports on the "autopsies" he performed on churches that died and found that they all shared one thing in common: they had turned their focus inward. They had turned a blind eye to changes that were happening in their surrounding community and made little effort to interact with new neighbors. There were no community-focused ministries. The church budget was solely focused on members' needs, and there were more and more arguments about what they—the members—wanted. As a result, they lost any sense of mission and purpose, decreased in membership, increased in age, and ended up idolizing previous eras until their doors closed for good.

The next generation of Catholics will need to be better at having an outward focus. Pope Francis continually speaks of a church that goes out to the peripheries and accompanies people. Too often, we create boundaries between insiders and outsiders and devote all our time, energy, and resources to those on the inside. By contrast, Jesus sent his disciples out beyond the boundaries that customarily kept the Jewish people insulated from those around them. The next generation of Catholics will need to recapture this missionary spirit and venture forth beyond the customary boundaries and focus on the needs of people at the peripheries.

They Will Need to Be Better at Reaching Men

Women are typically better at adapting to traditionally male environments than men are at adapting to traditionally female environments. For example, while many women often go to bars or stadiums to root for professional (men's) sports teams, many men avoid going to a baby shower like the plague.

For a variety of reasons, men have increasingly begun to see church as a feminine venue. This may seem strange because the hierarchy of the Catholic Church is completely male. However, if you take a close look, the majority of people in the pews and in ministries are women. Upwards of 80 percent of lay ecclesial ministers in the United States are laywomen and women religious. When I served as a catechist, I was always in the minority as a man. When I participated in a program to earn a certificate in spiritual direction, I was the only male in a group of seventeen. This gender gap is strangely peculiar to Christianity.

> For a variety of reasons, men have increasingly begun to see church as a feminine venue.

In his book *Why Men Hate Going to Church*, David Murrow explains that, from the moment men walk into church, they pick up subtle signals that they have entered feminine territory: images of Jesus that depict him as soft and meek; flowers, banners, and pastel colors; invitations to hold hands; songs that are too high to sing and contain lyrics about loving Jesus; and invitations to nurturing ministries. The next generation of Catholics will need to be better at using images that resonate with men and help them pay closer attention to their spirituality and embrace roles in ministry.

Till When the Soil Tells You It's Time

Professional gardeners know that the best time to till the soil is when the soil tells you it's time. In other words, the gardener needs to examine the soil to determine if it needs to be tilled. They do this by taking a handful of soil, squeezing it into a ball, and then pressing a finger slightly against the ball. If the ball crumbles because it is dry and compacted, it is time to till. Not all soil needs to be tilled. And some soil needs to be tilled more deeply than others.

As we seek to prepare people's hearts and minds, we too need to "listen to the soil." We need to pay close attention to those entrusted to us in faith formation so that we can respond in a manner that will resonate with them and their circumstances, thus allowing the seeds of God's Word to take root and yield a harvest.

The New Evangelization will not be powered by TV ads, print ads, billboards, or social media advertising. It will be accomplished by ordinary, everyday people who are not afraid of getting their fingernails dirty by tilling the soil and planting seeds—by sharing their stories of how living as a disciple of Jesus Christ has transformed their lives and enabled them to live a better way.

> The New Evangelization will be accomplished by ordinary, everyday people who are not afraid of getting their fingernails dirty by tilling the soil and planting seeds.

True Tales

People who know me well know that I am passionate about raising up young talent in ministry and that I delight in the success of up-and-coming pastoral ministers, especially in the field of catechesis, the part of God's vineyard where I have joyfully toiled for more than forty years. Several years ago, Loyola Press invited me to write a book about the spirituality of the catechist, and they encouraged me to identify a woman who could coauthor with me, because the majority of catechists are women. I thought for about five seconds before I blurted out the name of Julianne Stanz from the Diocese of Green Bay, Wisconsin, who is about twenty-five years my junior. Together, we collaborated on what became a very successful book, *The Catechist's Backpack: Spiritual Essentials for the Journey*, and we began taking the show on the road, doing presentations on the topic of the spirituality of the catechist. These experiences led to more and more invitations for Julianne to do presentations on a variety of topics in dioceses all over the country. A friend of mine who noticed this happening asked, "Aren't you worried that Julianne is going to steal the spotlight from you?" I laughed and said, "Of course not! I'm absolutely delighted to see her star on the rise. I've had my fifteen minutes of fame; it's time for a new generation of leaders to step up." Since then, I have had the joy of collaborating with numerous other, up-and-coming catechetical "stars," and I delight in seeing each and every one of them shine.

> When I'm six feet under, I'll rest in peace knowing that the sound I hear above me will be the sound of the next generation of catechetical ministers tilling the soil.

And when I'm six feet under, I'll rest in peace knowing that the sound I hear above me will be the sound of the next generation of catechetical ministers tilling the soil.

Questions for Reflection and Discussion

> When have you acted as a "customer evangelist," persuading someone to purchase a product or service that you had previously purchased?
> What difference does it make to think of those we teach not as students but as partners and coworkers whom we are apprenticing?
> What causes a church to die? Why is having an outward focus so critical to survival as a church?
> How do you view the relationship between faith and science? Has this been a stumbling block for you? Why or why not?
> Where have you experienced cultural diversity? How can people of various ethnicities reveal aspects of God we may not have been aware of?
> Who is someone who made faith relevant to you? How did they accomplish this?
> Who is someone who placed expectations on you to embrace the responsibilities that come with discipleship?
> Who is someone whose success you delight in because you were a part of their development and growth?

Scripture

Therefore go and make disciples of all nations, baptizing them in the name of the Father and of the Son and of the Holy Spirit, and teaching them to obey everything I have commanded you. And surely I am with you always, to the very end of the age.
MATTHEW 28:19–20

Prayer

Almighty and ever-living God, thank you for sending us your Son, Jesus, to teach us how to live in your image and likeness. May the Holy Spirit continue to inspire me, my fellow catechists, and all those we teach to prepare our hearts and minds so that the Living Word may take root and yield an abundant harvest. Amen.

BIBLIOGRAPHY

Berger, Jonah. *Contagious: Why Things Catch On.* New York, NY: Simon & Schuster, 2013.

Brown, Barbara Taylor. *Speaking of Sin: The Lost Language of Salvation.* Lanham, MD: Cowley Publications, 2000.

Catechism of the Catholic Church. Second Edition. Vatican: Libreria Editrice, Vaticana, 2000.

Congregation for the Clergy. *General Directory for Catechesis.* Washington, D.C.: United States Conference of Catholic Bishops, January 15, 1997. www.vatican.va.

Dillon, Christine. *Stories Aren't Just for Kids: Busting 10 myths about Bible storytelling.* Amazon Digital Services, LLC, 2017.

——*Telling the Gospel Through Story: Evangelism That Keeps Hearers Wanting More.* Downers Grove, IL: Intervarsity Press, 2012.

Donovan, Jeremey. *How to Deliver a TED Talk: Secrets of the World's Most Inspiring Presentations.* Lexington, KY: Self-published, 2012.

Evangelii Nuntiandi. Apostolic Exhortation, Pope Paul VI, 1975.

Fleming, David L. *What Is Ignatian Spirituality?* Chicago, IL: Loyola Press, 2008.

Go and Make Disciples: A National Plan and Strategy for Catholic Evangelization in the United States. United States Conference of Catholic Bishops, 1993.

Green, Charles H. *Trust-Based Selling: Using Customer Focus and Collaboration to Build Long-Term Relationships.* New York, NY: McGraw-Hill Education, 2005.

Halbach, Matthew. "New Pope, New Evangelization, New Return to Old (but Good) Ideas." *Catechetical Leader,* September 2013, Volume 24, Number 5.

——"What Parables Can Teach the Synod Fathers and the Church Today." *Catechetical Leader*, March 2015, Volume 26, Number 2.

Huba, Jackie, and Ben McConnell. *Creating Customer Evangelists: How Loyal Customers Become a Volunteer Salesforce.* Chicago, IL: Dearborn Trade Publishing, 2003

Kanaat, Robert. "Setting S.M.A.R.T.E.R. Goals: 7 Steps to Achieving Any Goal." Source: https://www.wanderlustworker.com/setting-s-m-a-r-t-e-r-goals-7-steps-to-achieving-any-goal/

Manney, Jim. *What Do You Really Want? St. Ignatius Loyola and the Art of Discernment.* Chicago, IL: Loyola Press, 2015.

Murrow, David. *Why Men Hate Going to Church.* Nashville, TN: Thomas Nelson, 2011.

Paprocki, Joseph. *A Church on the Move: 52 Ways to Get Mission and Mercy in Motion.* Chicago, IL: Loyola Press, 2016.

——*7 Keys to Spiritual Wellness: Enriching Your Faith by Strengthening the Health of Your Soul.* Chicago, IL: Loyola Press, 2012.

——*Living the Sacraments: Finding God at the Intersection of Heaven and Earth.* Chicago, IL: Loyola Press, 2018.

Rainer, Thom. *Autopsy of a Deceased Church: 12 Ways to Keep Your Church Alive.* Nashville: B&H Publishing Group, 2014.

Rite of Christian Initiation for Adults: Study Edition. International Commission on English in the Liturgy and Bishops Committee on the Liturgy, National Conference of Catholic Bishops, Chicago, IL: Liturgy Training Publications, 1998.

The Roman Missal, ICEL, 2012.

Shea, John. *An Experience Named Spirit.* Allen, TX: Thomas More, 1996.

——*Stories of Faith.* Chicago, IL: Thomas More, 1980.

Sinek, Simon. "Why Good Leaders Make You Feel Safe." TED

——*Start with Why: How Great Leaders Inspire Everyone to Take Action.* London, England: Penguin Books: 2009.

Teresa of Ávila. *The Collected Works of St. Teresa of Ávila (Vol. II)* including *The Interior Castle.* Washington, DC: ICS Publications, 1980.

Theophan the Recluse. "1st Homily on Prayer" Delivered November 21, 1864, Translated from the Russian by Rev. Father Michael van Opstall – January 2007, Source: http://www.monachos.net/content/patristics/patristictexts/228-theophan-prayer1

Warren, Cortney S. "Music Is What Feelings Sound Like." *Psychology Today*, October 23, 2014.

Westerhoff III, John H. *Will Our Children Have Faith?* (Third Revised Edition). New York, NY: Morehouse Publishing, 2012.

Wright, N.T. *Simply Jesus: A New Vision of Who He Was, What He Did, and Why He Matters.* New York, NY: Harper One, 2011.

Other Books in **The Toolbox Series**

The Catechist's Toolbox

How to Thrive as a Religious Education Teacher

English: PB | 978-0-8294-2451-5 | $9.95
Spanish: PB | 978-0-8294-8294-2767-7 | $9.95

The Catechist's Backpack

Spiritual Essentials for the Journey

English: PB | 978-0-8294-4246-5 | $9.95
Spanish: PB | 978-0-8294-4421-6 | $9.95

The Bible Blueprint

A Catholic's Guide to Understanding and Embracing God's Word

English: PB | 978-0-8294-2898-8 | $9.95
Spanish: PB | 978-0-8294-2858-2 | $9.95

A Well-Built Faith

A Catholic's Guide to Knowing and Sharing What We Believe

English: PB | 978-0-8294-2757-8 | $9.95
Spanish: PB | 978-0-8294-3299-2 | $9.95

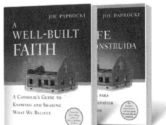

To Order: Call **800.621.1008**, visit **loyolapress.com/store**, or visit your local bookseller.

Other Books in **The Toolbox Series**

Beyond the Catechist's Toolbox

Catechesis That Not Only Informs but Also Transforms

English: PB | 978-0-8294-3829-1 | $7.95
Spanish: PB | 978-0-8294-3882-6 | $7.95

Practice Makes Catholic

Moving from a Learned Faith to a Lived Faith

English: PB | 978-0-8294-3322-7 | $9.95

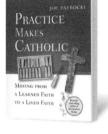

Living the Sacraments

Finding God at the Intersection of Heaven and Earth

English: PB | 978-0-8294-4659-3 | $11.95
Spanish: PB | 978-0-8294-4866-5 | $11.95

To Order: Call **800.621.1008**, visit **loyolapress.com/store**, or visit your local bookseller.

Also by **Joe Paprocki**

Handwritten annotations:
Acct # IRA # 72515827 71
ND # 600697185
1/14/22 11:57 Julie 33273 Primerica
Per share $1348.06
$329.25

A Church on the Move

52 Ways to Get Mission and Mercy in Motion

This practical resource for parishes includes 52 specific and achievable strategies to help Catholic parishes embody mission, mercy, and evangelization.

PB | 978-0-8294-4405-6 | $15.95

Handwritten: Temp PIN # 490462

7 Keys to Spiritual Wellness

Enriching Your Faith by Strengthening the Health of Your Soul

Discover a prescription for spiritual health based on the rich wisdom of Catholic Tradition with best-selling author Joe Paprocki as your guide.

PB | 978-0-8294-3689-1 | $12.95

Handwritten: Primerica.com right mutual fund Sign On Below

Under the Influence of Jesus

The Transforming Experience of Encountering Christ

Open yourself to encountering Christ, learn to live the Gospel, and evolve into a model of faith inspired by the Holy Spirit by reading the wisdom of Joe Paprocki in *Under the Influence of Jesus*.

English: PB | 978-0-8294-4050-8 | $15.95
Spanish: PB | 978-0-8294-4211-3 | $15.95

Handwritten: Begin new access PW Date of Birth

Living the Mass

How One Hour a Week Can Change Your Life

Accompanied by Fr. Dominic Grassi, Joe Paprocki illustrates how the one hour at Mass on Sunday can transform the other 167 hours of the week.

English: PB | 978-0-8294-3614-3 | $13.95
Spanish: PB | 978-0-8294-3758-4 | $13.95

To Order: Call 800.621.1008, visit **loyolapress.com/store**, or visit your local bookseller.